Table of Contents

Introduction 5
Adversity and the Human Spirit 5
The Power of Turning Points 9
Lessons on Personal Growth 14
Chapter 1: Immigrant Rebirth Stories 19
Leaving the Past Behind 19
Overcoming Obstacles 23
Embracing New Cultures 28
Paying Traditions Forward 33
Chapter 2: Tales of Professional Reinvention 40
Career Transitions 40
Discovering Hidden Passions 48
Acting on Purpose 56
Imparting Hard-Won Wisdom 65
Chapter 3: Entrepreneurial Metamorphosis Stories
.... 74
Spark of Business Idea 74
Setbacks to Success 83
Leadership Through Crisis 92
Uplifting Local Communities 100
Chapter 4: Second Chance Tales 109
Despair to Hope 109
Redemption and Forgiveness 115
Valuable Perspectives Gained 122
Making Amends Through Service 129

Chapter 5: Wellness Transformation Journeys....136
Health Crises.. 136
Commitment to Healing....................................... 144
Funding Research... 152
Helping Others Find Wholeness 162
Chapter 6: Environmental Activist Awakenings ... 171
Warnings Unheeded..171
Devastation Witnessed.. 180
Power of Protest 188
Sustainability as Mission 195
Chapter 7: Education Against Odds Stories 202
Barriers to Learning 202
Perseverance Paving Opportunity 209
Paying Fortune Knowledge Forward................. 216
Elevating Forgotten Voices 224
Conclusion 231
The Ripple Effects of Transformation 231
Internal Rebirth Reflects External Change 237
Growth Mindsets Fuel Positive Progress 244
Wordbook 251
Supplementary Materials 256

Copyright © 2023 by Sophia M. Johnson (Author)

All rights reserved. No part of this book may be reproduced or utilized in any form or by any means, electronic or mechanical, including photocopying, recording or by any information storage and retrieval system, without permission in writing from the publisher, except for brief quotations in critical articles or reviews.

The content of this book is based on various sources and is intended for educational and entertainment purposes only. While the author has made every effort to ensure the accuracy, completeness, and reliability of the information provided, the information may be subject to errors, omissions, or inaccuracies. Therefore, the author makes no warranties, express or implied, regarding the content of this book.

Readers are advised to seek the guidance of a licensed professional before attempting any techniques or actions outlined in this book. The author is not responsible for any losses, damages, or injuries that may arise from the use of information contained within. The information provided in this book is not intended to be a substitute for professional advice, and readers should not rely solely on the information presented.

By reading this book, readers acknowledge that the author is not providing legal, financial, medical, or professional advice. Any reliance on the information contained in this book is solely at the reader's own risk.

Thank you for selecting this book as a valuable source of knowledge and inspiration. Our aim is to provide you with insights and information that will enrich your understanding and enhance your personal growth. We appreciate your decision to embark on this journey of discovery with us, and we hope that this book will exceed your expectations and leave a lasting impact on your life.

Title: Stories of Resilience: Journeys of Hope and Growth
Subtitle: Turning Points of Transformation

Series: Worldwide Wellwishes: Cultural Traditions, Inspirational Journeys and Self-Care Rituals for Fulfillment in the Coming Year
Author: Sophia M. Johnson

Introduction
Adversity and the Human Spirit

In the intricate tapestry of human existence, adversity stands as an unwavering thread, weaving its way through the lives of individuals across cultures, continents, and epochs. It is a universal force that, in its myriad forms, has the power to shape destinies, redefine identities, and test the mettle of the human spirit. This introduction seeks to explore the profound connection between adversity and the indomitable resilience of the human spirit, setting the stage for the poignant stories of hope and growth that will unfold in the subsequent chapters.

Adversity, often regarded as an unwelcome intruder into the realms of our lives, is, paradoxically, an elemental force that catalyzes transformation. It is within the crucible of challenges and trials that the human spirit discovers its true strength, resilience, and capacity for growth. As we delve into the realms of personal narratives in the chapters that follow, the contours of this intricate dance between adversity and the human spirit will become vividly apparent.

The human spirit, that intangible force dwelling within each of us, is an extraordinary reservoir of courage, tenacity, and adaptability. It is a force that, when confronted with adversity, refuses to be extinguished. Instead, it rises to the occasion, drawing strength from the depths of the soul to navigate the stormy seas of life. Adversity becomes the crucible in which the human spirit is tested, refined, and ultimately forged into a more resilient, compassionate, and enlightened entity.

As we embark on this exploration of the human experience, it is essential to acknowledge the diverse forms that adversity can assume. Whether it manifests as the challenges faced by immigrants in unfamiliar lands, the upheavals of professional reinvention, the crucible of entrepreneurial pursuits, the redemption sought in second chances, the transformative journey through wellness crises, the awakening of environmental activists, or the pursuit of education against formidable odds, adversity wears many faces. It is through these varied lenses that we glimpse the myriad ways in which the human spirit responds to the call of resilience.

The power of turning points, those pivotal moments that stand as both catalysts and crucibles, will be a recurring theme in the stories that unfold. These turning points serve as the fulcrum upon which individuals pivot from despair to hope, from stagnation to growth. They are the junctures at which the human spirit asserts its innate ability to transcend circumstances, rewrite narratives, and emerge stronger, wiser, and more compassionate.

In the pages that follow, we will traverse the globe, exploring the personal journeys of individuals who have faced adversity in its various forms. From immigrant communities forging new identities to professionals navigating career metamorphoses, from entrepreneurs turning setbacks into success stories to individuals granted second chances seeking redemption, and from those overcoming health crises to environmental activists awakening to their mission — each narrative will be a testament to the enduring spirit of humanity in the face of adversity.

Through these stories, we will witness not only the trials and tribulations but also the triumphs and transformations that adversity begets. These narratives are not just tales of personal growth; they are chronicles of the human spirit's triumph over adversity — a celebration of resilience, forgiveness, and the pursuit of dreams against all odds.

As we embark on this journey, let us open our hearts and minds to the profound lessons that adversity imparts. Let us explore the intricate dance between challenge and growth, between despair and hope, and between adversity and the unyielding spirit that resides within us all. These are the stories of resilience, the journeys of hope and growth, and the turning points of transformation that define the human experience.

The Power of Turning Points

In the symphony of life, there exists a profound melody played by the cadence of pivotal moments — those junctures where destinies pivot, narratives transform, and the latent power of the human spirit unfurls. This section of the introduction delves into the essence of these turning points, exploring how they act as catalysts for growth, redemption, and ultimate transformation. As we embark on this exploration, the narratives to follow will be illuminated by the recognition that within the crucible of adversity, turning points emerge as both crucibles and liberators, wielding the power to alter the trajectory of one's journey.

Turning points are the fulcrum upon which the balance of life teeters, defining the very essence of our personal narratives. They are the moments of decision, the crossroads where individuals confront choices that shape the course of their lives. In the pages that follow, we will unravel the significance of these turning points, those singular instances when individuals stand at the precipice of change, confronted by the imperatives of choice and the potential for profound transformation.

These moments of inflection, often born out of adversity, serve as crucibles that test the resilience of the human spirit. They are the forks in the road where individuals face the stark reality of their circumstances, and it is in these moments that the latent strength of the human spirit is summoned. Turning points demand introspection, courage, and the willingness to embrace change, even when it unfolds in the guise of adversity.

Consider the immigrant who, leaving behind the familiar shores of their homeland, stands on the threshold of a new beginning in a foreign land. The decision to embark on such a journey is a turning point, a moment when the inertia of the past is disrupted, and the individual is propelled into the unknown. It is a choice laden with challenges, yet within its crucible lies the potential for rebirth, cultural assimilation, and the creation of a new identity.

Similarly, in the realm of professional reinvention, individuals often reach a juncture where the pursuit of passion supersedes the comfort of familiarity. The decision to transition careers, to delve into uncharted territories, is a turning point that tests one's resolve, adaptability, and resilience. It is a choice that can lead to the discovery of hidden talents, the fulfillment of long-suppressed aspirations, and the crystallization of purpose.

Entrepreneurial journeys, too, are punctuated by turning points — moments when the spark of an idea is ignited, setbacks are transformed into stepping stones, and leadership is forged in the crucible of crisis. The entrepreneur's odyssey is rife with choices that define the trajectory of their venture, and it is within these choices that the power of turning points is most palpable.

Second chances, often sought in the aftermath of despair, are epitomized by turning points that illuminate the path from darkness to redemption. The individual, having faced the consequences of past actions, is presented with a choice — to succumb to the weight of regret or to embark on a journey of transformation. This turning point becomes a compass guiding the way to forgiveness, self-discovery, and the restoration of a sense of purpose.

Wellness transformation journeys, marked by health crises, are navigated by individuals who reach turning points where the commitment to healing overrides the acceptance of illness. The decision to embark on a path of physical and mental well-being is a turning point that signifies the triumph of the human spirit over the adversity of illness. It is a choice to embrace life with renewed vigor and to extend a helping hand to others on similar journeys.

Environmental activists, too, are spurred to action by turning points — moments of awakening when the devastation wrought by environmental degradation becomes an undeniable call to arms. The decision to become an advocate for sustainability, to protest against heedless exploitation, is a turning point that transforms individuals into stewards of the planet. It is a choice to amplify the voices of the voiceless Earth and effect change on a global scale.

In the realm of education against formidable odds, turning points are the milestones that mark the triumph of perseverance over adversity. The barriers to learning, whether imposed by societal norms, economic constraints, or systemic inequalities, are confronted at crucial junctures. These turning points become the stepping stones to educational attainment, and more significantly, they pave the way for the elevation of forgotten voices.

As we traverse these diverse narratives, it is essential to recognize that turning points are not mere plot devices; they are crucibles of transformation. They are the moments when the human spirit confronts adversity and, in doing so, discovers its latent strength, resilience, and capacity for growth. Turning points embody the power of choice — the ability to transcend circumstances, rewrite narratives, and emerge on the other side, transformed.

The narratives that follow in the subsequent chapters will be imbued with the resonance of these turning points. Each story will be a testament to the profound impact of choices made in the face of adversity, illustrating how these moments of decision shape destinies, redefine identities, and propel individuals on journeys of hope and growth.

As we delve into the rich tapestry of these narratives, let us reflect on our own turning points — those moments in our lives when the choices we made, or failed to make, altered the course of our journey. Through the exploration of turning points in the lives of others, may we find inspiration, insight, and perhaps a renewed appreciation for the transformative power inherent in the choices we face, the decisions we make, and the resilience of the human spirit in the face of adversity.

Lessons on Personal Growth

In the expansive landscape of human experience, personal growth emerges as the verdant terrain where seeds of resilience, nurtured by adversity and guided by the compass of turning points, blossom into profound transformations. This section of the introduction delves into the essence of personal growth, weaving together the threads of individual narratives to distill lessons that resonate universally. As we embark on this exploration, the narratives to unfold will serve as poignant illustrations of the lessons drawn from diverse journeys of hope, adversity, and ultimate transformation.

Personal growth, often spoken of in hushed tones as an elusive pursuit, is the silent force that propels individuals towards becoming the architects of their own destinies. It is the journey of self-discovery, the evolution of character, and the continuous expansion of one's capacities. Within the crucible of adversity and the crucible of turning points, personal growth emerges as the verdant oasis—a testament to the extraordinary potential residing within each human spirit.

Consider the immigrant forging a new life in unfamiliar territory, encountering cultures and customs that stand as both challenges and opportunities. In the crucible of this experience, personal growth takes root. Lessons of adaptability, cultural empathy, and the resilience to face the unknown become the currency of their journey. The immigrant's story becomes a tapestry woven with threads of personal growth, as they evolve from individuals seeking refuge to architects of a new identity.

Professional reinvention, too, is a canvas upon which lessons of personal growth are painted. The individual transitioning from one career to another is not merely changing jobs; they are engaging in a profound metamorphosis. Lessons abound in the discovery of untapped passions, the courage to step into unfamiliar territory, and the wisdom gained from navigating uncharted waters. Personal growth, in this context, is the art of embracing change, cultivating adaptability, and discovering the boundless potential within.

Entrepreneurial pursuits, marked by setbacks and successes, are fertile grounds for lessons on personal growth. The entrepreneur, facing the uncertainties of business, learns the art of resilience, the value of strategic foresight, and the importance of leadership through adversity. Each trial becomes a masterclass, each triumph a validation of personal growth. The journey of entrepreneurship is, in essence, a perpetual quest for self-mastery and the cultivation of an indomitable spirit.

Second chances, sought in the wake of despair and redemption, offer profound lessons in personal growth. The individual, facing the consequences of past actions, learns the transformative power of forgiveness, the humility that comes with redemption, and the capacity to rise from the ashes of one's mistakes. The journey from despair to hope becomes a pilgrimage of self-discovery, each step a lesson etched in the annals of personal growth.

Wellness transformation journeys, often spurred by health crises, unfold as a curriculum in the school of personal growth. The individual navigating the labyrinth of illness learns the resilience of the body, the fortitude of the mind, and the interconnectedness of physical and mental well-being. Personal growth, in this context, is the evolution from a state of vulnerability to one of empowerment, a journey of healing that extends beyond the individual to inspire others on similar paths.

Environmental activists, awakening to the imperative of sustainability, glean lessons in personal growth amidst the challenges they confront. The devastation witnessed becomes a call to action, and the commitment to protest and advocate for the planet becomes a lesson in global citizenship. Personal growth, in the realm of environmental activism, is the deepening awareness of interconnectedness and the recognition that individual actions reverberate on a planetary scale.

Education against formidable odds, where barriers to learning are dismantled through perseverance and resilience, imparts invaluable lessons in personal growth. The individual who surmounts societal norms, economic constraints, and systemic inequalities learns the transformative power of education. Personal growth, in this context, is the journey from the margins to the center, the elevation of forgotten voices, and the recognition that knowledge is a catalyst for personal and societal transformation.

As we delve into these narratives of personal growth, it is crucial to recognize that the lessons drawn are not prescriptive but rather illuminative. Each story is a testament to the uniqueness of the human journey, a revelation of the myriad ways in which individuals navigate challenges and embrace growth. The lessons on personal growth are as diverse as the stories themselves, yet they converge on the universal truth that adversity, turning points, and the resilience of the human spirit are the crucibles where these lessons are forged.

The narratives that follow will be imbued with the richness of these lessons, each story offering insights into the transformative power of personal growth. From the immigrant learning to navigate a new cultural landscape to the entrepreneur leading through crisis, from the individual granted a second chance seeking redemption to the environmental activist advocating for a sustainable future — each narrative will serve as a prism refracting the lessons learned on the journey of personal growth.

As readers traverse these diverse stories, may they find resonance with the lessons drawn, discovering threads of commonality woven into the unique tapestry of each narrative. May these stories inspire self-reflection, ignite the flame of resilience, and foster a deep appreciation for the boundless potential within every human spirit. For, in the crucible of adversity and the crucible of turning points, the lessons on personal growth become a compass guiding individuals towards the transformative destination of their own becoming.

Chapter 1: Immigrant Rebirth Stories
Leaving the Past Behind

In the tapestry of human history, the narrative of immigration is a profound and universal one — a story of leaving behind the familiar, crossing borders, and stepping into the unknown in pursuit of a new beginning. The immigrant's journey is not merely a physical relocation but a transformative odyssey marked by the courage to sever ties with the past, confront the uncertainties of the present, and carve a new identity in an unfamiliar land. This chapter delves into the first subtopic, "Leaving the Past Behind," exploring the emotional and psychological dimensions of the immigrant experience and the profound lessons embedded in the act of relinquishing the known for the promise of the unknown.

The decision to migrate, to embark on a journey of immigration, is a momentous turning point — a choice that echoes across generations, reshaping destinies and redefining identities. It is, at its core, an act of leaving the past behind, a courageous step into the uncharted territories of possibility. The immigrant, in embracing this journey, confronts the inevitability of change and, in doing so, initiates a process of rebirth — a shedding of old skins to make way for new beginnings.

Leaving the past behind is a multifaceted process, one that involves not only physical relocation but also a profound emotional and psychological metamorphosis. The immigrant, bidding farewell to the familiar landscapes of home, severs the umbilical cord that ties them to the past. It is a poignant farewell to the sights, sounds, and smells that constitute the tapestry of childhood memories, familial ties, and cultural roots. The act of leaving is an act of surrender, a relinquishing of the known for the allure of the unknown.

This relinquishment is not without its emotional weight. It involves bidding farewell to the comforting embrace of familiar faces, the shared histories of communities, and the cultural tapestry that defines one's sense of self. The immigrant leaves behind the echoes of laughter, the cadence of native languages, and the comforting familiarity of traditions. The act of leaving is, in essence, a journey of disentanglement from the intricacies of the past, a necessary yet poignant prelude to the rebirth that awaits in a new land.

For many immigrants, leaving the past behind is not only about physical departure but also a departure from societal norms, expectations, and limitations. It is an emancipation from the constraints that may have defined their lives in their countries of origin — be it economic constraints, social expectations, or limitations imposed by systemic inequalities. The immigrant, in crossing borders, confronts the opportunity to redefine not only their geographical location but also the parameters that shape their aspirations, identities, and sense of agency.

This act of leaving, however, is not a singular event but a series of incremental farewells — a gradual unburdening of the baggage of the past. It involves shedding preconceived notions, unlearning biases, and releasing the grip of historical narratives that may have constrained personal growth. The immigrant's journey is, in many ways, a pilgrimage of self-discovery, a process of reimagining one's identity in a context that transcends the confines of the past.

The immigrant's arrival in a new land marks the beginning of a rebirth, a phoenix-like emergence from the ashes of the past. It is a process of shedding the skins of familiarity to embrace the unfamiliar, a psychological metamorphosis that demands resilience, adaptability, and an openness to change. The immigrant, having left the past behind, stands at the threshold of the unknown — a blank canvas upon which the narrative of their future is yet to be written.

In navigating this terrain of new beginnings, the immigrant encounters a myriad of challenges and opportunities. The unfamiliarity of the landscape, the nuances of a new culture, and the complexities of assimilation become both the crucible of adversity and the canvas for personal growth. Lessons learned in the act of leaving the past behind become the guiding stars, illuminating the path to resilience, adaptability, and the creation of a new identity.

The immigrant's journey is a testament to the indomitable spirit that propels individuals to leave behind the comfort of the known for the promise of the unknown. In relinquishing the past, the immigrant opens themselves to the transformative power of change — a change that encompasses not only geographical relocation but, more significantly, a change in mindset, perspective, and the very essence of self.

As we delve into the immigrant rebirth stories in the chapters that follow, the resonance of "Leaving the Past Behind" will echo through each narrative. From the poignant farewells to the emotional upheavals, from the challenges of assimilation to the triumphs of cultural integration — each story will be a chapter in the saga of rebirth, a testament to the resilience of those who dared to leave the past behind and, in doing so, discovered the boundless potential of the human spirit in the embrace of the unknown.

Overcoming Obstacles

In the intricate dance of immigration, the journey of leaving the past behind is often met with a myriad of obstacles that stand as formidable gatekeepers to the promise of a new beginning. This chapter delves into the subtopic of "Overcoming Obstacles," exploring the resilience, tenacity, and unwavering spirit exhibited by immigrants as they navigate the hurdles inherent in the pursuit of a better life. From bureaucratic challenges to cultural clashes, economic hardships to linguistic barriers, the immigrant's odyssey is a testament to the indomitable human spirit's ability to triumph over adversity.

The immigrant's journey, inherently marked by the act of leaving the past behind, becomes a crucible of challenges as they encounter the formidable obstacles that dot the landscape of relocation. These challenges, both anticipated and unforeseen, become the litmus test for the immigrant's resilience and determination to overcome the odds stacked against them.

One of the initial obstacles faced by many immigrants is the bureaucratic labyrinth that greets them upon arrival in a new land. Navigating visa processes, residency requirements, and documentation demands a level of bureaucratic acumen that can be overwhelming for those unfamiliar with the intricacies of a new system. The immigrant, confronted with the red tape that accompanies legal processes, must summon the patience and persistence to maneuver through these administrative mazes.

Economic hardships often loom large as a significant obstacle in the immigrant's path. The pursuit of financial stability in a new country can be a daunting task, especially when faced with the reality of initial unemployment or underemployment. The immigrant, often possessing skills and qualifications that may not be immediately recognized in their new environment, is compelled to confront the economic disparities that can hinder the realization of their aspirations. Overcoming this financial hurdle requires resourcefulness, adaptability, and a willingness to embrace opportunities that may lie outside one's preconceived career trajectory.

Cultural clashes become another prominent obstacle in the immigrant's journey. The collision of cultural norms, values, and expectations can create a dissonance that reverberates through various facets of life — from interpersonal relationships to workplace dynamics. The immigrant, caught between the gravitational forces of their cultural heritage and the demands of assimilation, must navigate this terrain with cultural intelligence and an openness to understanding and respecting differences.

Linguistic barriers present yet another hurdle in the immigrant's quest for integration. The mastery of a new language is not merely a linguistic challenge but a key that unlocks doors to social, professional, and educational opportunities. The immigrant, grappling with the complexities of a new language, faces the daunting task of overcoming communication barriers, asserting themselves in unfamiliar environments, and bridging the gap between their cultural identity and the linguistic demands of their adopted home.

Family dynamics, too, can pose significant obstacles. The immigrant, often uprooting not only themselves but also their families, must navigate the complexities of familial adjustments to a new cultural context. The challenges faced by children in adapting to new educational systems, the strains on familial bonds, and the renegotiation of roles within the family structure become additional layers in the immigrant's journey. Overcoming these familial challenges requires a delicate balance between preserving cultural identity and embracing the opportunities that come with cultural integration.

Discrimination and prejudice, unfortunately, remain pervasive obstacles faced by many immigrants. The immigrant, marked by visible or invisible differences, may encounter bias in various forms — be it racial, ethnic, or cultural. Overcoming these prejudices demands fortitude, advocacy, and a commitment to challenging stereotypes. The immigrant becomes not only a participant in their personal journey but also a trailblazer challenging societal norms and fostering a more inclusive environment for those who follow.

The immigrant's journey is replete with instances of overcoming adversity, and each obstacle surmounted becomes a testament to the strength of the human spirit. The stories of immigrants who navigate these challenges with resilience and determination are not merely tales of personal triumph; they are narratives that contribute to the broader narrative of societal evolution. The immigrant, in overcoming obstacles, becomes a catalyst for change, challenging the status quo and enriching the cultural fabric of their adopted home.

As we immerse ourselves in the immigrant rebirth stories in the chapters that follow, the echoes of "Overcoming Obstacles" will resound through each narrative. From the bureaucratic mazes to economic uncertainties, from cultural clashes to linguistic barriers, each story will be a testament to the indomitable spirit that propels individuals to triumph over adversity. These narratives will illuminate not only the challenges faced but also the invaluable lessons learned, the bridges built, and the transformative power inherent in the act of overcoming obstacles on the journey to a new beginning.

Embracing New Cultures

In the intricate mosaic of immigrant experiences, the act of leaving the past behind and overcoming obstacles paves the way for a profound and transformative journey — the embrace of new cultures. This chapter delves into the subtopic of "Embracing New Cultures," exploring the rich tapestry of encounters, adaptations, and the interplay between the immigrant's cultural heritage and the vibrant nuances of their adopted home. From culinary explorations to festive celebrations, from linguistic assimilation to the appreciation of diverse traditions, the immigrant's odyssey becomes a narrative of cultural fusion and a celebration of the diversity that enriches the fabric of their rebirth.

Embracing a new culture is a dynamic process that transcends the mere acquisition of surface-level customs; it involves a deep and reciprocal exchange that reshapes both the immigrant and the cultural context they enter. It is a dance between preservation and adaptation, a delicate interplay that sees the immigrant infusing their cultural identity into the mosaic of their adopted home while absorbing the myriad hues of the new culture.

Culinary exploration stands as one of the initial forays into the heart of a new culture. The immigrant, guided by the aromas wafting from local markets and the sizzle of street food stalls, embarks on a gastronomic adventure that transcends the mere consumption of sustenance. Food becomes a gateway to cultural understanding, a medium through which the immigrant not only nourishes their body but also fosters a connection to the culinary traditions of their new community.

Language, a vessel of cultural expression, becomes a focal point in the immigrant's journey of cultural assimilation. The mastery of a new language is not only a pragmatic necessity but a key to unlocking the richness of cultural nuances. Through language, the immigrant delves into the intricacies of local expressions, idioms, and the subtle cadences that shape interpersonal communication. The journey of linguistic assimilation is not just about acquiring a new set of words; it is an immersion into the soul of a culture, a bridge that connects the immigrant to the narratives, histories, and collective consciousness of their new community.

Cultural celebrations and festivals offer another dimension to the immigrant's exploration of their adopted home. From Diwali to Thanksgiving, Chinese New Year to Independence Day, the immigrant becomes a participant in the festive tapestry of their new culture. These celebrations are not merely events on the calendar but windows into the values, traditions, and shared experiences that bind communities together. The immigrant, through their involvement in cultural festivities, not only embraces new traditions but also contributes their unique perspectives, enriching the collective experience.

Navigating social norms and etiquette becomes an integral aspect of cultural assimilation. The immigrant, guided by a deep respect for the customs of their new community, learns the unspoken rules that govern social interactions. From greetings and gestures to workplace etiquette, the immigrant's journey involves a subtle negotiation between the familiar and the unfamiliar, as they integrate into the social fabric of their adopted home.

Educational and professional contexts offer immersive environments for the immigrant to deepen their engagement with the new culture. In classrooms and workplaces, the immigrant encounters diverse perspectives, collaborative methodologies, and professional norms that may differ from those in their country of origin. The embrace of these cultural nuances becomes a catalyst for personal growth, professional development, and the formation of connections that transcend cultural boundaries.

The immigrant's journey of embracing new cultures is a dynamic process of self-discovery and mutual enrichment.

It involves not only the adaptation of the immigrant to their new cultural context but also the reciprocal influence of the immigrant's cultural heritage on the communities they join. The exchange is symbiotic, fostering an environment where diversity is not merely tolerated but celebrated as a source of strength and collective growth.

In this cultural fusion, the immigrant becomes a cultural ambassador, a bridge between worlds. Their journey is marked by moments of cultural exchange — the sharing of traditional recipes, the storytelling of ancestral histories, and the celebration of customs that traverse geographical boundaries. The immigrant's unique perspective and cultural background contribute to the kaleidoscope of experiences that shape the collective identity of their adopted community.

As we immerse ourselves in the immigrant rebirth stories in the chapters that follow, the echoes of "Embracing New Cultures" will resonate through each narrative. From the vibrant hues of cultural celebrations to the shared meals that become a communion of traditions, from linguistic assimilation to the navigation of social norms — each story will be a testament to the transformative power of cultural exchange. These narratives will illuminate not only the challenges faced in embracing new cultures but also the beauty and richness inherent in the confluence of diverse traditions, creating a mosaic that is more vibrant, resilient, and inclusive.

Paying Traditions Forward

In the intricate tapestry of immigrant rebirth stories, the thread of cultural legacy intertwines with the narratives of leaving the past behind, overcoming obstacles, and embracing new cultures. This chapter delves into the subtopic of "Paying Traditions Forward," exploring how immigrants, fueled by the profound respect for their cultural heritage, become stewards of traditions, custodians of ancestral wisdom, and architects of a cultural legacy that transcends geographical borders. From familial rituals to community engagements, from the preservation of language to the transmission of values, the immigrant's journey becomes a narrative of continuity — a legacy paid forward for future generations.

The immigrant, having left behind the landscapes of their homeland, carries within them the seeds of cultural traditions that have been nurtured over generations. The act of paying traditions forward is not merely a preservation effort; it is a dynamic engagement that involves the adaptation of traditions to new environments, the transmission of cultural values, and the contribution of unique perspectives to the evolving narrative of their adopted community.

Preserving Family Traditions

For many immigrants, the family becomes the sacred vessel through which cultural traditions are safeguarded and passed on to future generations. The immigrant household becomes a microcosm of cultural continuity, where familial rituals, celebrations, and daily practices become the living threads that connect the past to the present. From the preparation of traditional meals to the observance of religious ceremonies, the immigrant family becomes the custodian of a cultural legacy, paying traditions forward with each passing day.

Family storytelling becomes a powerful means of preserving and transmitting cultural values. Immigrant parents, grandparents, and elders become the oral historians, weaving tales of ancestral lands, historical events, and the resilience of their people. Through these narratives, the younger generations gain insights into their cultural roots, forging a connection to a heritage that may span continents. The immigrant's living room becomes a classroom where history is not merely recounted but lived through the stories that echo with the wisdom of the past.

Language as a Cultural Beacon

The preservation and propagation of language stand as pivotal elements in the immigrant's journey of paying traditions forward. Language is not merely a tool for communication; it is a repository of cultural nuances, a vessel that carries the collective wisdom, idioms, and expressions of a people. The immigrant, often bilingual or multilingual, becomes an ambassador for their native language, a custodian of linguistic traditions that bridge generations and continents.

The transmission of language occurs not only within the familial domain but extends to the broader community. Language classes, cultural schools, and community initiatives become conduits for the immigrant to share their linguistic heritage. In doing so, they pay traditions forward by ensuring that future generations retain the ability to communicate in the language of their ancestors. Language becomes a cultural beacon that illuminates the path to understanding, appreciation, and the perpetuation of a shared cultural identity.

Cultural and Religious Celebrations

Festivals and religious celebrations become vibrant expressions of cultural continuity in the immigrant's journey. From Diwali to Eid, Lunar New Year to Christmas, the immigrant community infuses the cultural landscape of their adopted home with the colors, flavors, and traditions of their heritage. These celebrations are not isolated events but become communal gatherings where the immigrant pays traditions forward by inviting others to partake in the richness of their cultural tapestry.

Religious institutions also play a crucial role in the immigrant's journey of cultural preservation. Places of worship become focal points for community engagement, where religious rituals, ceremonies, and congregational activities become conduits for the transmission of cultural values. The immigrant, whether attending a mosque, temple, church, or synagogue, contributes to the vitality of these institutions, paying traditions forward by fostering a sense of community that transcends cultural and geographical boundaries.

Cultural Arts and Crafts

Artistic expressions, including music, dance, and visual arts, become powerful means through which immigrants pay traditions forward. Traditional art forms, whether rooted in classical styles or folk traditions, find new life in the diaspora. The immigrant, be they a musician, dancer, painter, or storyteller, becomes a custodian of artistic traditions, infusing creativity with cultural resonance.

Cultural festivals and community events become stages for the immigrant to showcase their artistic heritage. From traditional dance performances to musical concerts, from art exhibitions to storytelling sessions, the immigrant pays traditions forward by sharing the beauty and richness of their cultural arts. In doing so, they contribute not only to the preservation of artistic traditions but also to the cultural diversity that enhances the collective human experience.

Community Engagement and Philanthropy

The immigrant's journey of paying traditions forward extends beyond familial and cultural contexts to broader community engagement. Many immigrants actively participate in philanthropic initiatives, contributing to charitable organizations, community development projects, and initiatives that address social issues. In doing so, they pay traditions forward by embodying cultural values such as compassion, community support, and social responsibility.

Community organizations and cultural associations become focal points for the immigrant to actively contribute to the well-being of their adopted community. Whether through volunteerism, mentorship programs, or initiatives that promote cross-cultural understanding, the immigrant becomes an agent of positive change, paying traditions forward by embodying the values instilled by their cultural heritage.

Mentorship and Education

Education becomes a key arena where immigrants pay traditions forward. The immigrant, often valuing the transformative power of knowledge, becomes an advocate for education within their community. Mentorship programs, scholarship initiatives, and educational outreach efforts become vehicles through which the immigrant empowers younger generations to pursue academic excellence while instilling the values of their cultural heritage.

The immigrant's journey of paying traditions forward involves not only transmitting knowledge but also fostering a growth mindset that encourages continuous learning and adaptation. Education becomes a dynamic bridge between cultural continuity and the evolving landscape of the immigrant's adopted home.

Navigating Generational Shifts

As traditions are paid forward, the immigrant encounters the dynamic interplay between generational shifts and cultural evolution. The second and third generations, born or raised in the adopted country, navigate a cultural landscape that is shaped not only by their ancestral heritage but also by the influences of the broader society. The immigrant, in paying traditions forward, must navigate the delicate balance between preserving cultural identity and allowing for the organic evolution of traditions within the context of a changing world.

This navigation involves open dialogues between generations, an acknowledgment of the diverse perspectives that may emerge, and a commitment to fostering a sense of cultural pride and belonging. The immigrant's journey of paying traditions forward becomes a collaborative effort, where the wisdom of the older generations converges with the fresh perspectives of the younger ones, creating a continuum of cultural heritage that remains vibrant, relevant, and adaptive.

In conclusion, the act of paying traditions forward becomes a transformative journey within the immigrant narrative. It is a dynamic engagement with the past, present, and future — a commitment to cultural continuity that enriches not only the immigrant's life but also the broader tapestry of their adopted community. As we delve into the immigrant rebirth stories in the chapters that follow, the echoes of "Paying Traditions Forward" will resonate through each narrative. From familial rituals to community engagements, from the preservation of language to the transmission of values — each story will be a testament to the enduring legacy of immigrants who, in paying traditions forward, become architects of a cultural heritage that transcends borders and generations.

Chapter 2: Tales of Professional Reinvention
Career Transitions

In the dynamic landscape of professional reinvention, the chapter on "Career Transitions" unveils a myriad of stories where individuals, driven by a desire for fulfillment and purpose, navigate the challenging terrain of shifting from one career trajectory to another. This chapter delves into the intricacies of the professional metamorphosis experienced by these individuals, exploring the motivations, challenges, and ultimate triumphs as they navigate uncharted waters and redefine their paths in the pursuit of professional satisfaction.

Motivations for Change

The decision to embark on a career transition is often fueled by a complex interplay of motivations, a realization that the current professional trajectory no longer aligns with one's passions, values, or aspirations. Tales of professional reinvention often begin with a stirring within—an acknowledgment that there exists a misalignment between the individual's authentic self and the demands of their current career.

Motivations for career transitions vary widely. Some individuals seek to escape the monotony of a job that no longer challenges or inspires them, while others may be driven by a quest for personal fulfillment and a deeper sense of purpose. The desire to make a meaningful impact, contribute to a cause, or pursue a long-held passion becomes a magnetic force pulling individuals toward the unexplored territories of new career possibilities.

For many, the recognition that life is finite acts as a catalyst for change. The ticking clock becomes a constant reminder that spending the majority of waking hours in a profession that does not bring joy or satisfaction is a disservice to one's own potential. Career transition, in this context, becomes a conscious choice to reclaim agency over one's professional narrative and chart a course that aligns more authentically with one's values and aspirations.

Navigating Uncertainty

The path of career transition is seldom a linear trajectory. It is a journey marked by uncertainties, risks, and the inherent challenges of venturing into the unknown. Navigating uncertainty becomes a defining aspect of tales of professional reinvention, as individuals grapple with the ambiguity of their chosen path and confront the fear of stepping out of their comfort zones.

The uncertainty often arises from factors such as financial risks, the prospect of starting anew in a different industry, or the fear of societal judgment. The individual in the midst of a career transition must grapple with questions about financial stability, the potential need for additional education or training, and the resilience required to weather the inevitable setbacks that accompany professional reinvention.

Moreover, the societal expectation of a linear career trajectory adds an additional layer of uncertainty. Straying from the conventional path can evoke skepticism from others, leading individuals to confront not only their own doubts but also the judgments and perceptions of those around them. Tales of professional reinvention, therefore, often involve navigating societal expectations, overcoming external pressures, and cultivating the internal fortitude to persevere in the face of uncertainty.

The Courage to Begin Again

Embarking on a career transition requires a profound degree of courage—the courage to acknowledge that change is necessary, the courage to confront fears and uncertainties, and the courage to take the first step into uncharted professional territory. The tales of individuals who find the courage to begin again are narratives of resilience, determination, and the unwavering belief in the possibility of a more fulfilling professional future.

The decision to begin again may involve returning to school, acquiring new skills, or gaining experience in a different industry. It requires a willingness to embrace a novice's mindset, to be humble in the face of unfamiliar challenges, and to accept that the journey of professional reinvention is, in many ways, a process of continual learning and growth.

Beginning again is not just a practical step; it is a psychological and emotional commitment to a new vision of professional success. It involves shedding the identity associated with the previous career, navigating the discomfort of being a beginner, and embracing the vulnerability that comes with starting anew. The courage to begin again is, therefore, a transformative act that goes beyond the external trappings of a career change—it is a profound redefinition of self.

Embracing Hidden Passions

Tales of professional reinvention often unfold as journeys of self-discovery, where individuals uncover hidden passions and talents that were overshadowed or neglected in their previous professional pursuits. The act of embracing hidden passions becomes a central theme in these narratives, as individuals discover that their true calling may lie in realms they had not previously considered.

Hidden passions can range from creative pursuits like art, writing, or music to entrepreneurial endeavors, social impact initiatives, or even pursuits in academia. The revelation of these passions often occurs during the process of self-reflection that precedes a career transition. The individual may recognize a yearning for creative expression, a desire to make a positive impact, or a fascination with a field of knowledge that had been relegated to the sidelines.

Embracing hidden passions becomes a transformative force, infusing the journey of professional reinvention with a sense of purpose and authenticity. Individuals who recognize and act upon their hidden passions often find that their work becomes more than just a means of livelihood—it becomes a source of joy, fulfillment, and alignment with their true selves.

Acting on Purpose

Purpose becomes a guiding star in tales of professional reinvention. Individuals who undergo career transitions often seek work that aligns with a deeper sense of purpose—a mission or cause that transcends the narrow confines of a job description. Acting on purpose involves aligning one's professional endeavors with values, beliefs, and a vision of contributing to something larger than oneself.

The pursuit of purpose may lead individuals to non-profit organizations, social enterprises, or fields where the impact on societal or environmental issues is central. It may involve a shift towards careers that emphasize personal growth and well-being, where the individual sees their work as a means of making a positive contribution to the world.

Acting on purpose is not merely about finding a job that feels meaningful; it is about infusing every aspect of professional life with intentionality. From daily tasks to long-term goals, individuals who act on purpose bring a sense of mindfulness and dedication to their work. The pursuit of purpose becomes a compass that guides decisions, inspires perseverance in the face of challenges, and fosters a deeper connection to the broader impact of one's professional contributions.

Imparting Hard-Won Wisdom

The tales of professional reinvention are not only stories of personal triumph but also narratives rich with hard-won wisdom. Individuals who navigate the twists and turns of career transitions accrue a wealth of insights, lessons, and practical wisdom that often become valuable guideposts for others contemplating similar journeys.

Imparting hard-won wisdom involves sharing the challenges faced, the strategies employed to overcome obstacles, and the mindset shifts that proved pivotal in the process of reinvention. It becomes a form of mentorship, where individuals who have successfully navigated career transitions offer support, advice, and encouragement to those at the early stages of contemplating change.

The act of imparting hard-won wisdom also extends beyond individual mentorship to contribute to the broader discourse on professional reinvention. Individuals who have undergone career transitions may become advocates for workplace flexibility, champions of alternative career paths, or contributors to conversations around the evolving nature of work. In doing so, they play a crucial role in shaping societal attitudes toward diverse career trajectories and fostering a culture that embraces the value of professional reinvention.

In conclusion, the subtopic of "Career Transitions" within the chapter on "Tales of Professional Reinvention" is a narrative tapestry woven with threads of motivation, courage, self-discovery, and the pursuit of purpose. As we delve into the stories of individuals who have navigated the complexities of reshaping their professional paths, we encounter not only the challenges and uncertainties inherent in career transitions but also the profound transformations that occur when individuals dare to align their work with their authentic selves. Each tale becomes a testament to the resilience of the human spirit, the capacity for growth and adaptation, and the enduring belief that it is never too late to embark on a journey of professional reinvention.

Discovering Hidden Passions

Within the labyrinth of professional reinvention lies a transformative journey of self-discovery—an exploration that often leads individuals to uncover hidden passions that have remained dormant or overlooked in the course of their professional lives. The chapter on "Discovering Hidden Passions" delves into narratives where individuals, propelled by a desire for authenticity and fulfillment, embark on a quest to unearth talents, interests, and creative pursuits that may have been obscured by the demands of their previous careers. These tales illuminate the process of discovering hidden passions as a profound act of self-revelation, leading to career trajectories that resonate with a newfound sense of purpose.

The Awakening

The journey of discovering hidden passions often begins with a subtle awakening—an internal recognition that something essential is missing from one's professional life. Individuals experiencing this awakening may find themselves questioning the alignment between their current career and their deepest desires. It could manifest as a restlessness, a yearning for something more, or a realization that the routine of their daily work no longer sparks the enthusiasm it once did.

This awakening is a pivotal moment—an invitation to introspection and self-inquiry. Individuals grappling with the awakening may embark on a process of reflection, asking themselves fundamental questions about their values, aspirations, and the activities that bring them genuine joy. This internal dialogue becomes the compass guiding them towards the discovery of hidden passions that may hold the key to a more fulfilling professional journey.

Reconnecting with Childhood Dreams

For some individuals, the journey of discovering hidden passions involves revisiting the dreams and aspirations of their childhood. As responsibilities, societal expectations, and the practicalities of adulthood take center stage, the whimsical dreams of youth often recede into the background. However, the call to discover hidden passions often rekindles the flame of these childhood dreams, prompting individuals to reconsider pursuits that once held immense significance.

The reconnection with childhood dreams may involve rekindling artistic endeavors, exploring scientific curiosities, or delving into hobbies and interests that were set aside in pursuit of more conventional career paths. In these narratives, individuals rediscover the joy and authenticity embedded in pursuits that may have been dismissed as impractical or fanciful in the pragmatic landscape of adulthood.

Unveiling Creative Expressions

The discovery of hidden passions frequently manifests through creative expressions. Individuals navigating professional reinvention may find solace, joy, and a sense of purpose in creative outlets such as writing, painting, music, or other artistic endeavors. The act of creating becomes a means of self-discovery, allowing individuals to tap into wellsprings of imagination, emotion, and self-expression that may have been untapped in their previous careers.

For some, the process of unveiling creative expressions involves experimenting with various art forms, attending workshops, or collaborating with like-minded individuals. The journey becomes an exploration of the limitless possibilities that creativity offers and an acknowledgment that the pursuit of hidden passions often leads to the unearthing of unique, artistic talents.

Pursuing Entrepreneurial Ventures

The discovery of hidden passions sometimes propels individuals toward entrepreneurial ventures. The entrepreneurial spirit, ignited by the desire to turn a passion into a profession, becomes a driving force in the process of professional reinvention. Individuals who embark on this path often recognize that their hidden passions can be transformed into not just personal fulfillment but also viable business opportunities.

Entrepreneurial ventures arising from the discovery of hidden passions may involve launching creative businesses, establishing niche services, or developing products that align with the individual's authentic interests. These ventures become a manifestation of the individual's commitment to crafting a professional life that integrates passion, purpose, and autonomy.

Navigating Fear and Resistance

While the discovery of hidden passions can be exhilarating, it is often accompanied by fear and resistance. The transition from a familiar career to the pursuit of newfound passions requires individuals to confront uncertainties, step outside their comfort zones, and grapple with the fear of the unknown. Navigating this fear becomes a crucial aspect of the journey, as individuals must reconcile their aspirations with the practicalities of making a living and sustaining themselves in a new professional landscape.

Resistance may also arise from external factors, such as societal expectations, financial concerns, or the opinions of friends and family. Individuals discovering hidden passions may find themselves contending with questions and skepticism from those who perceive such pursuits as risky or unconventional. Overcoming this resistance involves cultivating resilience, self-belief, and a steadfast commitment to the authenticity of the chosen path.

Balancing Passion and Practicality

Discovering hidden passions often leads to a delicate balancing act between the pursuit of personal fulfillment and the practicalities of making a living. Individuals navigating this terrain must consider how to integrate their passions into a sustainable professional model—one that aligns with their values while addressing the practical aspects of financial stability and career longevity.

The quest for balance may involve strategic planning, financial preparation, and a phased approach to integrating newfound passions into one's professional life. It requires a pragmatic assessment of the skills and resources needed to turn passions into viable careers, as well as a commitment to continuous learning and adaptation in the face of evolving challenges.

Creating a Portfolio Career

For some individuals, the journey of discovering hidden passions unfolds as a process of creating a portfolio career. A portfolio career involves combining multiple professional pursuits and income streams that align with an individual's diverse skills and interests. This approach allows individuals to cultivate a multidimensional professional life that accommodates their newfound passions alongside other complementary activities.

The creation of a portfolio career often involves freelancing, consulting, or pursuing part-time work in addition to dedicating time to passion-driven projects. This flexibility enables individuals to craft a professional narrative that reflects the richness and diversity of their skills and interests. It becomes a dynamic response to the discovery of hidden passions, allowing individuals to curate a professional life that evolves with their changing aspirations.

Contributing to Social Impact

The discovery of hidden passions frequently intersects with a desire to contribute to social impact and positive change. Individuals uncovering passions that align with societal or environmental issues often seek ways to integrate their professional pursuits with a broader mission. This may involve transitioning to careers in social entrepreneurship, nonprofit work, or other fields where the individual's skills and passions can be harnessed for the greater good.

Contributing to social impact becomes a powerful motivator, transforming the journey of discovering hidden passions into a vehicle for meaningful change. Individuals who align their passions with a commitment to societal well-being often find a profound sense of purpose, knowing that their professional endeavors contribute not only to personal fulfillment but also to the betterment of the broader community.

The Ongoing Journey of Exploration

The journey of discovering hidden passions is not a finite destination but an ongoing exploration. As individuals integrate their newfound pursuits into their professional lives, they often find that the process of self-discovery continues to unfold. The dynamic nature of passions, evolving interests, and changing aspirations requires individuals to remain open to new possibilities, embrace continuous learning, and adapt their professional trajectories in response to internal and external shifts.

The ongoing journey of exploration involves a commitment to self-reflection, curiosity, and the willingness to pivot when necessary. Individuals discovering hidden passions become lifelong learners, navigating the ever-changing landscape of their authentic selves and actively shaping their professional narratives to reflect the evolving dimensions of their passions.

Conclusion: A Symphony of Self-Discovery

In the chapter on "Discovering Hidden Passions," the tales of professional reinvention weave a symphony of self-discovery, resilience, and the transformative power of aligning one's professional pursuits with authentic passions. As we delve into the narratives of individuals who have embarked on this journey, we encounter not only the exhilaration of uncovering hidden talents but also the challenges, fears, and triumphs inherent in the pursuit of a professional life infused with purpose and authenticity. Each tale becomes a testament to the limitless possibilities that arise when individuals dare to explore the depths of their authentic selves, revealing the hidden passions that have the potential to shape and enrich their professional destinies.

Acting on Purpose

In the captivating tapestry of professional reinvention, the subtopic of "Acting on Purpose" emerges as a pivotal theme, illuminating the narratives of individuals who, in the pursuit of authenticity and fulfillment, align their professional endeavors with a deeper sense of purpose. This chapter delves into stories where purpose becomes not just a guiding principle but a transformative force, propelling individuals to make deliberate choices that resonate with their values, beliefs, and a profound desire to contribute meaningfully to the world.

The Essence of Purpose in Professional Reinvention

At the heart of tales of professional reinvention lies the essence of purpose—an intrinsic motivator that transcends the conventional metrics of success. Purpose, in this context, refers to a deep understanding of one's core values, a clarity about the impact one wishes to make, and a commitment to aligning one's professional pursuits with a broader sense of meaning. Acting on purpose becomes a conscious and intentional choice, shaping the trajectory of professional reinvention with a sense of direction and significance.

The journey of acting on purpose often begins with self-reflection—an exploration of personal values, passions, and the impact one aspires to have on the world. Individuals seeking to infuse purpose into their professional lives embark on an introspective quest to uncover the driving forces that underpin their sense of self and inform their aspirations. This self-awareness becomes the foundation upon which purpose is woven into the fabric of professional reinvention.

The Pursuit of Meaningful Impact

Acting on purpose entails a profound commitment to making a meaningful impact in the world. Individuals in the throes of professional reinvention often grapple with the question of how their skills, talents, and passions can be harnessed to contribute positively to society, the environment, or the well-being of others. The pursuit of meaningful impact becomes a driving force, infusing the journey of professional reinvention with a sense of significance and a desire to leave a lasting and positive legacy.

This pursuit may manifest in various forms, from engaging in socially responsible business practices to actively participating in initiatives that address societal challenges. Individuals acting on purpose seek to align their professional endeavors with a sense of responsibility, leveraging their skills and resources to create positive change in areas that resonate with their values and convictions.

Aligning Values with Professional Choices

The essence of purpose in professional reinvention is intricately tied to the alignment of values with professional choices. Individuals on this transformative journey recognize the importance of congruence between their personal convictions and the decisions they make in their professional lives. Acting on purpose involves a conscious effort to ensure that every professional choice, from career transitions to daily work tasks, reflects and upholds the individual's deeply held values.

This alignment is not just an external display but a profound internal harmony. It involves an authenticity in the way individuals present themselves in professional settings, the relationships they cultivate, and the impact they seek to create. The process of aligning values with professional choices becomes a continuous navigation, requiring individuals to remain vigilant, adapt to changing circumstances, and make decisions that resonate with the ever-evolving understanding of their authentic selves.

Nurturing Intrinsic Motivation

Acting on purpose often nurtures intrinsic motivation—the internal drive that goes beyond external rewards and recognition. Individuals who infuse purpose into their professional lives find that their motivation extends beyond financial gain or societal approval. The pursuit of purpose becomes a source of intrinsic joy, satisfaction, and a deep sense of fulfillment derived from the alignment of one's work with a higher calling.

Nurturing intrinsic motivation involves cultivating a mindset that values the impact of one's contributions over external markers of success. It requires individuals to tap into the inherent joy derived from the act of creating, contributing, and making a difference. The narratives within this theme reveal how acting on purpose unlocks a wellspring of internal motivation that sustains individuals through the challenges of professional reinvention.

Transcending Conventional Definitions of Success

Acting on purpose often involves transcending conventional definitions of success. In the context of professional reinvention, success is not solely measured by traditional metrics such as salary, status, or job title. Instead, individuals guided by purpose redefine success to encompass the alignment of their work with their values, the positive impact they make, and the personal fulfillment derived from contributing to something greater than themselves.

This shift in perspective challenges societal norms and expectations, prompting individuals to question the established benchmarks of achievement. Tales within this theme unfold as narratives of individuals who courageously choose authenticity over conformity, significance over societal validation, and purpose over predetermined notions of success. The journey becomes a profound exploration of what it truly means to lead a successful and purpose-driven professional life.

Pivoting Towards Social Entrepreneurship

Acting on purpose often leads individuals towards the realm of social entrepreneurship—a space where profit and purpose coalesce to create sustainable and impactful ventures. Social entrepreneurs leverage business principles to address societal challenges, viewing their enterprises not only as economic entities but also as vehicles for positive change. Tales within this theme showcase individuals who pivot towards social entrepreneurship as a deliberate choice to align their professional endeavors with a commitment to social and environmental well-being.

These narratives unveil the complexities of navigating the intersection of profit and purpose. Social entrepreneurs face unique challenges, from balancing financial sustainability with social impact to establishing ethical and transparent business practices. The journey becomes a testament to the transformative potential of enterprises that prioritize purpose, demonstrating that businesses can be catalysts for positive change in the world.

Empowering Others Through Mentorship

The pursuit of purpose often extends beyond personal fulfillment to a commitment to empower others. Individuals acting on purpose recognize the importance of sharing their knowledge, experiences, and insights with those on similar journeys of professional reinvention. Mentorship becomes a powerful vehicle through which individuals contribute to the growth and success of others, fostering a sense of community and collective progress.

Empowering others through mentorship involves not only providing guidance but also creating a supportive and nurturing environment. Mentors within this theme share not only their successes but also their challenges and failures, offering a holistic view of the professional reinvention journey. The act of empowering others becomes a reciprocal exchange, enriching the mentor as they witness the growth and achievements of those they guide.

The Challenge of Balancing Profit and Purpose

Acting on purpose often poses the challenge of balancing profit and purpose—a delicate equilibrium that requires individuals to navigate the complexities of a world where financial sustainability is intertwined with societal impact. Tales within this theme explore the nuanced decisions individuals make as they seek to create businesses or pursue careers that generate profit while remaining true to their commitment to positive change.

The challenge of balancing profit and purpose involves strategic decision-making, ethical considerations, and a commitment to transparency in business practices. Individuals within this theme grapple with questions of how to generate revenue without compromising their values, how to scale their impact without diluting their mission, and how to foster a culture of purpose within their organizations.

Navigating Setbacks with Resilience

Acting on purpose does not shield individuals from setbacks and challenges. Instead, the narratives within this theme reveal how individuals navigate adversity with resilience, using setbacks as opportunities for growth and learning. The journey of professional reinvention is marked by twists and turns, and individuals acting on purpose approach challenges with a mindset that views obstacles not as roadblocks but as stepping stones toward greater resilience and wisdom.

Navigating setbacks with resilience involves a willingness to adapt, learn from failures, and persevere in the face of adversity. Individuals within this theme share stories of how setbacks became catalysts for innovation, refinement of purpose, and a deepening of their commitment to creating positive change. The tales become a testament to the inherent strength that arises when purpose becomes a guiding force in the face of adversity.

Fostering a Culture of Purpose in Organizations

For individuals who rise to leadership positions or establish their own organizations, acting on purpose extends to fostering a culture of purpose within the workplace. The narratives within this theme explore how individuals shape organizational cultures that prioritize values, ethical practices, and a commitment to positive societal impact. Creating a culture of purpose becomes a strategic imperative, attracting like-minded individuals and contributing to the long-term success and sustainability of the organization.

Fostering a culture of purpose involves intentional leadership, transparent communication, and the alignment of organizational goals with a broader mission. Individuals within this theme share how they navigate the challenges of balancing the demands of running a successful business with the imperative of maintaining a purpose-driven ethos. The stories become blueprints for organizations seeking to integrate purpose into their DNA.

Conclusion: The Transformative Power of Acting on Purpose

In the chapter on "Acting on Purpose," the tales of professional reinvention converge to reveal the transformative power of aligning one's professional endeavors with a deeper sense of purpose. As we immerse ourselves in the narratives of individuals who have made purpose a guiding force in their journey of reinvention, we witness not only the courage to defy conventional definitions of success but also the profound impact that arises when individuals commit to creating positive change in the world. Each story becomes a testament to the extraordinary possibilities that unfold when purpose becomes not just a concept but a lived experience, shaping the trajectory of professional lives with authenticity, meaning, and a deep sense of fulfillment.

Imparting Hard-Won Wisdom

In the labyrinthine landscape of professional reinvention, the subtopic of "Imparting Hard-Won Wisdom" emerges as a compelling theme, unveiling the narratives of individuals who, having weathered the storms of career transitions, offer invaluable insights, lessons, and practical wisdom to those embarking on similar journeys. This chapter delves into stories where the act of imparting hard-won wisdom becomes not only a personal catharsis but also a generous contribution to the broader discourse on professional reinvention, offering guidance, support, and a roadmap for navigating the complexities of reshaping one's professional path.

The Role of Mentorship in Professional Reinvention

Imparting hard-won wisdom often finds its expression through mentorship—a symbiotic relationship where individuals who have traversed the terrain of professional reinvention become guides and confidants to those at the nascent stages of their journeys. The role of mentorship extends beyond providing practical advice; it involves sharing personal experiences, empathizing with the challenges faced by mentees, and fostering a supportive environment where individuals can navigate the uncertainties of reinvention with confidence.

Mentorship within this theme is not a one-size-fits-all approach but a nuanced and personalized exchange. Mentors draw from their own stories of triumphs and setbacks, offering insights that transcend generic career advice. The narratives within this theme unfold as testimonials to the transformative power of mentorship, where the shared wisdom becomes a beacon of light, illuminating the path for those who seek guidance in the labyrinth of professional reinvention.

Navigating the Emotional Landscape of Change

One of the facets of imparting hard-won wisdom involves acknowledging and navigating the emotional landscape of change. Tales within this theme explore the emotional highs and lows that accompany professional reinvention—feelings of uncertainty, fear, excitement, and self-discovery. Individuals who have weathered these emotional storms offer insights into how to cultivate resilience, manage self-doubt, and embrace the transformative potential embedded in the emotional journey of change.

Navigating the emotional landscape involves not only recognizing the emotional toll of career transitions but also developing strategies for self-care, mindfulness, and maintaining a positive mindset. Mentors within this theme share how they confronted moments of doubt, faced fears of the unknown, and ultimately emerged with a deeper understanding of their own emotional resilience. The narratives serve as a guide for others, illustrating that the emotional aspect of professional reinvention is not a hindrance but a source of strength and growth.

Recognizing the Value of Adaptability

Imparting hard-won wisdom often emphasizes the intrinsic value of adaptability—a crucial attribute for individuals navigating the unpredictable currents of professional reinvention. Tales within this theme underscore the inevitability of change and the importance of cultivating a mindset that embraces adaptability as a cornerstone of success. Individuals who have undergone multiple career transitions share how their ability to adapt to evolving circumstances became a defining factor in their reinvention journeys.

Adaptability involves not only being open to change but actively seeking opportunities for growth and learning. Mentors within this theme encourage mentees to view challenges as opportunities, to pivot when necessary, and to approach their careers with a fluidity that allows for continuous evolution. The narratives become testimonials to the transformative power of adaptability, illustrating that the ability to navigate change with grace and resilience is a skill that can be honed and refined.

Embracing Lifelong Learning

A common thread within the narratives of imparting hard-won wisdom is the emphasis on embracing lifelong learning. The professional landscape is dynamic and ever-evolving, requiring individuals to remain curious, open to new experiences, and committed to ongoing education. Mentors within this theme share their experiences of pursuing additional education, acquiring new skills, and adapting to emerging trends in their respective fields.

Lifelong learning becomes a means of staying relevant and resilient in the face of changing professional landscapes. The narratives highlight the various ways individuals engage in continuous education, from formal academic pursuits to self-directed learning and skill-building. The act of imparting wisdom extends beyond providing answers to encouraging mentees to ask questions, seek knowledge, and cultivate a mindset of curiosity that fuels their professional growth.

Cultivating Resilience in the Face of Setbacks

Imparting hard-won wisdom often centers on the theme of resilience—a quality that proves indispensable when navigating the inevitable setbacks and challenges of professional reinvention. The narratives within this theme unfold as testimonials to the resilience demonstrated by individuals who faced setbacks, experienced failures, and emerged stronger on the other side.

Cultivating resilience involves reframing setbacks as opportunities for learning and growth. Mentors within this theme share how they navigated moments of uncertainty, job loss, or unexpected challenges and transformed these experiences into catalysts for reinvention. The stories become a source of inspiration, offering reassurance to those facing adversity that setbacks are not the end but a chapter in the larger narrative of professional growth.

Strategies for Effective Networking and Relationship Building

A critical aspect of imparting hard-won wisdom involves sharing strategies for effective networking and relationship building. The narratives within this theme explore the role of connections, mentorship, and professional relationships in the reinvention journey. Individuals who have successfully built meaningful networks offer insights into the art of cultivating relationships that can support and propel one's career forward.

Effective networking goes beyond accumulating contacts; it involves fostering genuine connections built on trust, mutual support, and shared values. Mentors within this theme encourage mentees to approach networking with authenticity, to actively seek out mentorship relationships, and to contribute to the professional community. The stories become a roadmap for those navigating the intricate web of professional relationships, illustrating that a well-crafted network can be a source of guidance, opportunities, and resilience.

Balancing Ambition with Realistic Expectations

An essential element of imparting hard-won wisdom is striking a balance between ambition and realistic expectations. Individuals who have undergone professional reinvention share insights into how they navigated the tension between ambitious career goals and the need for pragmatic decision-making. Mentors within this theme offer guidance on setting realistic expectations, making informed choices, and finding equilibrium between aspirations and the practicalities of the professional landscape.

Balancing ambition with realistic expectations involves self-awareness, an understanding of one's values and priorities, and the ability to recalibrate goals in response to changing circumstances. The narratives within this theme become a source of counsel for those grappling with the challenge of ambitious career pursuits, illustrating that success can be achieved through a combination of strategic ambition and a grounded understanding of the professional terrain.

Fostering a Growth Mindset

Imparting hard-won wisdom often centers on fostering a growth mindset—a belief that intelligence, abilities, and talents can be developed through dedication, learning, and perseverance. Mentors within this theme share how cultivating a growth mindset became a cornerstone of their reinvention journeys, enabling them to approach challenges as opportunities for learning and development.

Fostering a growth mindset involves reframing failures as opportunities for growth, viewing challenges as a natural part of the learning process, and maintaining a sense of curiosity and resilience in the face of setbacks. The narratives within this theme serve as a guide for individuals seeking to cultivate a growth mindset, illustrating that the ability to adapt, learn, and evolve is a powerful asset in the ever-changing landscape of professional reinvention.

The Importance of Building a Personal Brand

Imparting hard-won wisdom often underscores the importance of building a personal brand—a unique identity that distinguishes individuals in their professional spheres. Mentors within this theme share their experiences of crafting and refining their personal brands, offering insights into how a well-defined brand can enhance visibility, credibility, and career opportunities.

Building a personal brand involves a strategic and intentional approach to self-presentation. Mentors encourage mentees to identify their strengths, values, and unique contributions, and to communicate these aspects consistently across various professional platforms. The narratives within this theme become a playbook for those seeking to elevate their professional profiles, emphasizing that a well-crafted personal brand can open doors, attract opportunities, and shape the trajectory of one's reinvention journey.

Conclusion: The Enduring Legacy of Imparting Wisdom

In the chapter on "Imparting Hard-Won Wisdom," the narratives of professional reinvention weave a tapestry of resilience, growth, and the enduring legacy of individuals who generously share their insights with those navigating similar paths. As we immerse ourselves in the stories of mentors imparting hard-won wisdom, we witness not only the triumphs over challenges but also the profound impact that mentorship and shared experiences can have on the reinvention journey. Each narrative becomes a beacon, illuminating the way for others and affirming that the act of imparting wisdom is not just a personal catharsis but a timeless contribution to the collective knowledge of those who dare to reshape their professional destinies.

Chapter 3: Entrepreneurial Metamorphosis Stories
Spark of Business Idea

In the realm of entrepreneurial metamorphosis, the inception of a business idea is a moment of profound inspiration—a spark that ignites the journey of transformation from vision to reality. The subtopic "Spark of Business Idea" explores the narratives of individuals who, fueled by passion, insight, and a desire for innovation, embark on the exhilarating path of entrepreneurship. This chapter delves into stories where the inception of a business idea becomes a catalyst for metamorphosis, propelling individuals to navigate the complexities of turning their visions into thriving enterprises.

The Genesis of Innovation

The spark of a business idea often originates in the fertile soil of innovation—a willingness to question the status quo, identify unmet needs, and envision solutions that redefine industries. Tales within this theme unravel as narratives of individuals who observed gaps in the market, recognized untapped opportunities, or were inspired by a deep-seated passion to create something new and impactful.

The genesis of innovation involves a mindset that sees challenges as opportunities and views problems as invitations to innovate. Entrepreneurs within this theme share how they cultivated this mindset, honing their ability to identify problems worth solving and envisioning creative solutions that would resonate with their target audiences. The narratives serve as a testament to the transformative power of innovative thinking, illustrating that the inception of a business idea is often rooted in a commitment to pushing boundaries and imagining a better way.

Identifying Market Gaps and Unmet Needs

A common thread within the stories of entrepreneurial metamorphosis is the astute ability to identify market gaps and unmet needs. Entrepreneurs who successfully translate their business ideas into reality often share experiences of keen observation, market research, and a deep understanding of the needs and desires of their target customers.

Identifying market gaps involves a meticulous examination of existing products, services, or industries to pinpoint areas where improvements or alternatives are needed. Entrepreneurs within this theme recount how they conducted thorough market analyses, listened to customer feedback, and immersed themselves in the intricacies of their chosen sectors to uncover opportunities for innovation. The narratives become a guide for aspiring entrepreneurs, emphasizing the importance of perceptive observation and a customer-centric approach in the process of conceiving a business idea.

Passion as the Driving Force

The inception of a business idea is often intertwined with a driving force—passion. Entrepreneurs within this theme share how their deepest passions became the foundation upon which their business ideas were built. Whether driven by a love for a particular industry, a commitment to social or environmental causes, or a personal experience that ignited a fervor for change, these narratives illuminate the transformative energy that passion injects into the entrepreneurial journey.

Passion serves as a relentless motivator, propelling individuals to overcome obstacles, persist in the face of challenges, and stay committed to their visions. Entrepreneurs recount how their unwavering passion fueled their determination to bring their ideas to fruition, becoming a source of resilience in moments of uncertainty. The narratives serve as a testament to the enduring power of passion in entrepreneurial metamorphosis, illustrating that businesses built on genuine enthusiasm have the potential to not only survive but thrive.

From Problem Solving to Business Concept

The spark of a business idea often emerges from a process of problem-solving. Entrepreneurs within this theme recount how they encountered challenges or inefficiencies in their personal or professional lives and, inspired by the desire to find solutions, conceptualized businesses that addressed these issues.

The journey from problem-solving to a viable business concept involves the refinement of ideas, validation of solutions, and a strategic alignment with market demands. Entrepreneurs share how they iterated on their initial concepts, sought feedback from potential users, and fine-tuned their business models to create offerings that resonated with their target audiences. The narratives become a roadmap for individuals seeking to translate their problem-solving instincts into entrepreneurial ventures, illustrating that businesses born from authentic problem-solving have the potential to meet real-world needs.

The Serendipity of Creative Sparks

In some entrepreneurial metamorphosis stories, the spark of a business idea is serendipitous—a moment of unexpected inspiration that sets the course for a transformative journey. Entrepreneurs within this theme recount instances where chance encounters, unforeseen circumstances, or seemingly unrelated experiences sparked creative ideas that ultimately became the foundation of their businesses.

The serendipity of creative sparks involves a willingness to embrace unexpected insights and a receptiveness to inspiration from diverse sources. Entrepreneurs share how chance conversations, exposure to different cultures, or encounters with emerging technologies led to the formulation of innovative business ideas. The narratives serve as a reminder that creativity often thrives in the intersection of disparate elements, and entrepreneurs who remain open to serendipitous sparks may find unique and impactful avenues for their ventures.

Validating the Viability of Ideas

The inception of a business idea is only the beginning; its viability must be rigorously tested and validated. Entrepreneurs within this theme emphasize the importance of subjecting their ideas to thorough validation processes, ensuring that there is a demand for their products or services and that their concepts are economically feasible.

Validation involves gathering feedback from potential customers, conducting market research, and assessing the competitive landscape. Entrepreneurs share their experiences of adapting their ideas based on the insights gained during the validation process, refining their value propositions, and ensuring that their business concepts align with the needs and preferences of their target markets. The narratives become a guide for aspiring entrepreneurs, underscoring the significance of validating ideas before committing resources to their realization.

The Role of Intuition and Gut Feeling

In the midst of data-driven validation processes, entrepreneurs often emphasize the role of intuition and gut feeling in shaping their business ideas. While rigorous analysis is crucial, entrepreneurs within this theme share how their instincts played a significant role in guiding crucial decisions, particularly in situations where data was incomplete or ambiguous.

Intuition becomes a valuable compass, helping entrepreneurs navigate uncertainties, make informed judgments, and seize opportunities that may not be immediately evident through analytical processes alone. The narratives within this theme serve as a reminder that, alongside empirical validation, trusting one's instincts can be a powerful tool in the entrepreneurial toolkit, allowing individuals to make decisions that align with their vision and values.

The Collaborative Nature of Idea Generation

The spark of a business idea is often a collaborative endeavor, emerging from the intersection of diverse perspectives, skills, and experiences. Entrepreneurs within this theme share stories of how collaboration and collective brainstorming sessions played a pivotal role in the generation and refinement of their business concepts.

Collaborative idea generation involves fostering a culture of open communication, where team members are encouraged to share their insights, challenge assumptions, and contribute to the creative process. Entrepreneurs recount how diverse teams, with members possessing varied backgrounds and expertise, enriched the idea generation phase, bringing forth innovative solutions and ensuring a comprehensive exploration of possibilities. The narratives become a testament to the idea that the most impactful business ideas often arise from the synergy of collective intelligence.

Nurturing Ideas into Concrete Concepts

The journey from the spark of a business idea to a concrete and actionable concept involves deliberate nurturing and refinement. Entrepreneurs within this theme share how they translated their initial sparks into detailed business plans, outlining key components such as value propositions, revenue models, and go-to-market strategies.

Nurturing ideas into concrete concepts requires a methodical approach, involving market analysis, feasibility studies, and the development of a strategic roadmap. Entrepreneurs recount the iterative nature of this process, detailing how they refined their concepts based on feedback, market dynamics, and evolving industry trends. The narratives serve as a guide for individuals at the early stages of their entrepreneurial journeys, emphasizing the importance of meticulous planning and strategic thinking in transforming ideas into viable business concepts.

Conclusion: The Birth of Transformative Ventures

In the chapter on the "Spark of Business Idea," the narratives of entrepreneurial metamorphosis converge to illuminate the transformative power inherent in the inception of a business concept. As we delve into the stories of individuals whose ventures were ignited by sparks of inspiration, we witness not only the creative processes that gave rise to innovative ideas but also the strategic and collaborative efforts that nurtured these sparks into concrete and impactful business concepts. Each narrative becomes a beacon, inspiring aspiring entrepreneurs and affirming that the spark of a business idea is not just a fleeting moment of inspiration but the birth of ventures that have the potential to reshape industries, address societal needs, and leave enduring legacies in the world of entrepreneurship.

Setbacks to Success

In the dynamic landscape of entrepreneurial metamorphosis, the journey from ideation to realization is often marked by a series of setbacks that serve as crucibles for growth, resilience, and ultimate success. The subtopic "Setbacks to Success" delves into the narratives of entrepreneurs who, in the face of challenges, setbacks, and unforeseen obstacles, demonstrated the fortitude to navigate adversity and transform setbacks into stepping stones toward triumph. This chapter unravels stories of resilience, adaptability, and the indomitable spirit that propels individuals to overcome setbacks and carve out success in the entrepreneurial arena.

The Inevitability of Setbacks in Entrepreneurship

Entrepreneurial journeys are inherently characterized by uncertainty, ambiguity, and unforeseen challenges. The inception and growth of a business often unfold in uncharted territories, where the landscape is shaped by market dynamics, competition, and external factors beyond an entrepreneur's control. As we explore the narratives within this theme, a common thread emerges—the inevitability of setbacks in entrepreneurship.

Entrepreneurs share stories of encountering unforeseen obstacles, facing market downturns, and navigating the complexities of building a business from the ground up. Setbacks become a natural part of the entrepreneurial narrative, and the narratives within this theme serve as a testament to the resilience and adaptability required to transform setbacks into opportunities for learning and growth.

Learning from Failure

Setbacks, often synonymous with failure, become powerful catalysts for learning and growth in the entrepreneurial journey. Entrepreneurs within this theme recount experiences of ventures that did not unfold as initially envisioned, products that did not resonate with the market, or strategies that did not yield the expected results. However, these setbacks were not endpoints but rather pivotal moments of introspection and education.

Learning from failure involves a willingness to critically examine what went wrong, identify areas for improvement, and integrate these lessons into future endeavors. Entrepreneurs share how setbacks became invaluable sources of insight, enabling them to refine their business strategies, reassess market dynamics, and iterate on their approaches. The narratives become a guide for aspiring entrepreneurs, emphasizing that the ability to learn from failure is a hallmark of successful entrepreneurial journeys.

Adapting to Market Changes

The entrepreneurial landscape is dynamic, subject to constant shifts in market trends, consumer preferences, and technological advancements. Entrepreneurs within this theme share stories of setbacks stemming from changes in the market, whether due to economic downturns, shifts in consumer behavior, or the emergence of disruptive technologies.

Adapting to market changes involves a nimble and flexible approach to business strategies. Entrepreneurs recount experiences of pivoting their business models, diversifying product offerings, or exploring new markets in response to evolving circumstances. The narratives serve as a testament to the importance of adaptability in entrepreneurship, highlighting that setbacks can become opportunities for innovation and strategic repositioning in the face of dynamic market forces.

Resilience in the Face of Financial Challenges

Financial challenges often loom large in the entrepreneurial journey, and setbacks in this domain can be particularly daunting. Entrepreneurs within this theme share stories of facing financial setbacks, whether in the form of cash flow issues, fundraising challenges, or unexpected expenses. However, these setbacks become crucibles for resilience, resourcefulness, and financial acumen.

Resilience in the face of financial challenges involves creative problem-solving, strategic budgeting, and the ability to weather the storms of economic uncertainty. Entrepreneurs recount experiences of renegotiating contracts, seeking alternative funding sources, and making prudent financial decisions to navigate through periods of financial turbulence. The narratives become a source of inspiration for entrepreneurs facing similar challenges, illustrating that resilience is a foundational trait in transforming financial setbacks into sustainable success.

Navigating Leadership Challenges

Setbacks in entrepreneurship are often intertwined with leadership challenges, as entrepreneurs navigate the complexities of leading teams, making critical decisions, and fostering a positive organizational culture. Entrepreneurs within this theme share stories of setbacks related to leadership, whether stemming from communication breakdowns, team dynamics, or personal growth challenges.

Navigating leadership challenges involves introspection, continuous learning, and the development of effective leadership skills. Entrepreneurs recount experiences of seeking mentorship, investing in leadership development programs, and fostering open communication within their teams to address setbacks related to leadership. The narratives become a guide for entrepreneurs aspiring to cultivate effective leadership in the face of setbacks, emphasizing the transformative power of strong leadership in steering ventures toward success.

Overcoming Product Development Hurdles

In the journey from ideation to market launch, setbacks in product development can present formidable hurdles for entrepreneurs. Entrepreneurs within this theme share stories of setbacks related to product design, manufacturing issues, or unexpected technical challenges. However, these setbacks become pivotal moments for innovation, iterative design, and ultimately, the creation of products that meet market demands.

Overcoming product development hurdles involves a commitment to quality, a focus on user feedback, and a willingness to refine and enhance products based on real-world usage. Entrepreneurs recount experiences of collaborating with engineers, leveraging user testing, and embracing a mindset of continuous improvement to address setbacks in product development. The narratives serve as a guide for entrepreneurs navigating the intricacies of bringing innovative products to market, illustrating that setbacks can fuel a commitment to excellence in product creation.

The Role of Mentorship in Overcoming Setbacks

Mentorship emerges as a recurring theme in the narratives of overcoming setbacks in entrepreneurship. Entrepreneurs share stories of seeking guidance from mentors—experienced individuals who have weathered their own entrepreneurial storms and emerged with valuable insights. Mentors play a crucial role in providing perspective, offering advice, and serving as sounding boards during challenging times.

The role of mentorship in overcoming setbacks involves building relationships with mentors who can provide a balance of support and constructive criticism. Entrepreneurs recount experiences of learning from the mistakes and successes of their mentors, leveraging their networks, and benefiting from the wisdom gained through years of entrepreneurial experience. The narratives become a testament to the transformative power of mentorship, illustrating that having a guiding hand can be instrumental in navigating setbacks and steering toward success.

Pivoting as a Strategic Response to Setbacks

Pivoting—a strategic shift in business direction—is a common response to setbacks in entrepreneurship.

Entrepreneurs within this theme share stories of how setbacks prompted them to reassess their initial strategies, pivot their business models, and explore new avenues for growth.

Pivoting involves a blend of strategic vision, adaptability, and a keen understanding of market dynamics. Entrepreneurs recount experiences of rebranding, entering new markets, or exploring innovative partnerships as strategic responses to setbacks. The narratives become a guide for entrepreneurs facing challenges, illustrating that strategic pivots can be transformative, opening doors to new opportunities and ultimately leading to success.

Building a Resilient Organizational Culture

Setbacks in entrepreneurship are not solely individual challenges but also impact the organizational culture and dynamics of teams. Entrepreneurs within this theme share stories of setbacks that tested the resilience of their organizational cultures, requiring a collective commitment to weathering challenges and fostering a positive work environment.

Building a resilient organizational culture involves transparent communication, a focus on employee well-being, and a shared commitment to the overarching mission and values of the company. Entrepreneurs recount experiences of rallying their teams during challenging times, fostering a culture of open communication, and prioritizing the mental and emotional well-being of their employees. The narratives become a source of inspiration for entrepreneurs aspiring to build resilient organizations, emphasizing that a strong organizational culture is a cornerstone of overcoming setbacks and achieving sustainable success.

The Transformative Power of Perseverance

Perseverance emerges as a defining trait in the narratives of overcoming setbacks in entrepreneurship. Entrepreneurs share stories of facing moments of doubt, enduring sleepless nights, and navigating the emotional rollercoaster that often accompanies setbacks. However, through unwavering perseverance, they not only weathered the storms but emerged stronger and more resilient.

The transformative power of perseverance lies in the commitment to staying the course, even in the face of adversity. Entrepreneurs recount experiences of pushing through challenges, maintaining a positive mindset, and using setbacks as opportunities for personal and professional growth. The narratives become a testament to the enduring impact of perseverance in the entrepreneurial journey, illustrating that setbacks, when met with determination, can be transformative milestones on the path to success.

Conclusion: Triumph Beyond Setbacks

In the chapter on "Setbacks to Success," the narratives of entrepreneurial metamorphosis converge to illuminate the transformative journey from adversity to triumph. As we immerse ourselves in the stories of entrepreneurs who navigated setbacks with resilience, adaptability, and perseverance, we witness not only the challenges inherent in the entrepreneurial landscape but also the enduring spirit that propels individuals to transform setbacks into stepping stones toward success. Each narrative becomes a beacon, inspiring aspiring entrepreneurs and affirming that setbacks are not roadblocks but integral chapters in the narrative of triumph beyond adversity in the dynamic world of entrepreneurship.

Leadership Through Crisis

In the crucible of entrepreneurship, leaders are often defined not only by their successes but by their ability to navigate and lead through crises. The subtopic "Leadership Through Crisis" delves into the narratives of entrepreneurs who, faced with unforeseen challenges, demonstrated exceptional leadership acumen, resilience, and strategic thinking to steer their ventures through turbulent times. This chapter unveils stories of leadership tested by adversity, showcasing the transformative power of effective leadership in the entrepreneurial metamorphosis.

The Nature of Leadership in Entrepreneurship

Leadership in entrepreneurship goes beyond the conventional paradigms. Entrepreneurs within this theme share stories of leadership that is not just about making decisions but about embracing uncertainty, inspiring teams, and fostering a culture of adaptability. The nature of leadership in entrepreneurship involves a dynamic and agile approach, where leaders serve as visionaries, problem-solvers, and motivators in equal measure.

Leadership is tested most profoundly during crises, whether they arise from market downturns, unexpected challenges, or external disruptions. The narratives within this theme become a testament to the multifaceted nature of entrepreneurial leadership, illustrating that effective leaders not only navigate crises but also transform challenges into opportunities for growth and innovation.

Leading with Vision and Purpose

Effective leadership in times of crisis begins with a clear and compelling vision coupled with a strong sense of purpose. Entrepreneurs within this theme share stories of how their unwavering vision for their ventures and a deep sense of purpose guided them through tumultuous periods.

Leading with vision involves communicating a roadmap for the future, even when the path may seem uncertain. Entrepreneurs recount experiences of aligning their teams with a shared vision, articulating long-term goals, and fostering a collective sense of purpose that transcends immediate challenges. The narratives become a guide for entrepreneurs, emphasizing that visionary leadership provides a stable compass in the midst of uncertainty and crisis.

Effective Communication in Times of Uncertainty

Communication is a linchpin of effective leadership, especially in times of crisis. Entrepreneurs within this theme emphasize the role of transparent and empathetic communication in guiding their teams through challenging periods.

Effective communication involves not only disseminating information but also actively listening to concerns, addressing uncertainties, and fostering a culture of openness. Entrepreneurs share experiences of conducting regular updates, maintaining a transparent dialogue with their teams, and creating channels for feedback during times of crisis. The narratives serve as a reminder that clear and empathetic communication is a cornerstone of effective leadership, providing reassurance and guidance in uncertain times.

Embracing Adaptability as a Leadership Skill

Crisis often demands adaptability, and effective leaders in entrepreneurship are those who can pivot, innovate, and lead their teams through change. Entrepreneurs within this theme share stories of how they embraced adaptability as a leadership skill, steering their ventures through unforeseen challenges by fostering a culture of flexibility and resilience.

Adaptability involves not only reacting to crises but proactively seeking opportunities within them. Entrepreneurs recount experiences of empowering their teams to embrace change, iterating on business models, and pivoting strategies when necessary. The narratives become a guide for entrepreneurs aspiring to lead with adaptability, illustrating that resilience and flexibility are vital qualities for navigating the uncertainties of the entrepreneurial journey.

Building a Resilient Team Culture

Leadership through crisis extends beyond individual resilience to the cultivation of a resilient team culture. Entrepreneurs within this theme share stories of fostering a team culture that thrives in the face of adversity—a culture built on trust, collaboration, and a shared commitment to weathering challenges together.

Building a resilient team culture involves creating an environment where team members feel supported, empowered, and encouraged to contribute their best even in challenging circumstances. Entrepreneurs recount experiences of investing in team development, providing resources for skill-building, and fostering a sense of camaraderie that becomes a source of strength during crises. The narratives become a testament to the transformative impact of resilient team cultures, illustrating that effective leadership involves not just leading individuals but inspiring a collective resilience that can withstand challenges.

Strategic Decision-Making Under Pressure

Leadership in crisis requires the ability to make strategic decisions under pressure. Entrepreneurs within this theme share stories of navigating high-stakes decisions, whether related to financial restructuring, adapting business models, or reevaluating market strategies.

Strategic decision-making involves a blend of data-driven analysis, intuition, and a willingness to take calculated risks. Entrepreneurs recount experiences of seeking counsel, gathering diverse perspectives, and making decisions that align with their overarching vision and goals. The narratives become a guide for entrepreneurs facing moments of critical decision-making, emphasizing the importance of a strategic and measured approach in navigating crises.

Navigating Financial Challenges with Fiscal Prudence

Financial challenges often accompany crises in entrepreneurship, placing leaders in the role of financial stewards for their ventures. Entrepreneurs within this theme share stories of navigating financial challenges with fiscal prudence—making sound financial decisions to ensure the sustainability of their ventures during turbulent times.

Navigating financial challenges involves strategic budgeting, seeking alternative funding sources, and making decisions that prioritize long-term stability over short-term gains. Entrepreneurs recount experiences of managing cash flows, renegotiating contracts, and making tough financial decisions to safeguard the financial health of their ventures.

The narratives become a source of inspiration for entrepreneurs facing financial uncertainties, illustrating that leadership in crisis demands fiscal acumen and a commitment to long-term financial viability.

Crisis as an Opportunity for Innovation

Exceptional leaders view crises not just as challenges to overcome but as opportunities for innovation and growth. Entrepreneurs within this theme share stories of how they transformed crises into catalysts for innovation, whether by introducing new products, exploring untapped markets, or reimagining their business models.

Innovation in crisis involves a mindset that sees challenges as invitations to create and explore new possibilities. Entrepreneurs recount experiences of encouraging a culture of innovation within their teams, experimenting with new approaches, and leveraging crises as moments for transformative change. The narratives become a guide for entrepreneurs, illustrating that effective leadership involves not only weathering crises but harnessing them as springboards for innovation and evolution.

Leading with Empathy and Emotional Intelligence

Leadership through crisis is inherently human, requiring leaders to navigate not just the operational challenges but also the emotional landscape of their teams. Entrepreneurs within this theme emphasize the role of empathy and emotional intelligence in effective leadership during turbulent times.

Leading with empathy involves understanding and acknowledging the emotions of team members, providing support, and fostering a culture of compassion. Entrepreneurs share experiences of leading with emotional intelligence, recognizing the impact of crises on the well-being of their teams, and creating spaces for open dialogue and support. The narratives serve as a reminder that effective leadership is not just about steering through challenges but also about empathetically guiding individuals through the emotional nuances of uncertainty.

The Role of Mentorship in Leadership Development

Mentorship emerges as a recurring theme in the narratives of leadership through crisis. Entrepreneurs share stories of seeking guidance from mentors—experienced individuals who have navigated their own leadership challenges and emerged with valuable insights.

The role of mentorship in leadership development involves learning from the experiences of those who have faced similar challenges, receiving guidance on decision-making, and benefiting from the wisdom gained through years of leadership. Entrepreneurs recount experiences of mentorship shaping their leadership styles, providing valuable perspectives during crises, and offering a sounding board for critical decisions. The narratives become a testament to the transformative power of mentorship in leadership development, illustrating that having a guiding hand can be instrumental in navigating the complexities of leading through crises.

Conclusion: Leadership as the Beacon in the Storm

In the chapter on "Leadership Through Crisis," the narratives of entrepreneurial metamorphosis converge to illuminate the transformative role of effective leadership in navigating and triumphing over adversity. As we immerse ourselves in the stories of entrepreneurs who led with vision, adaptability, and resilience through crises, we witness not only the challenges inherent in leadership but also the enduring spirit that propels individuals to transform crises into opportunities for growth and innovation. Each narrative becomes a beacon, inspiring aspiring entrepreneurs and affirming that effective leadership is not just about steering through calm waters but about shining brightest when guiding through the storms of uncertainty in the dynamic world of entrepreneurship.

Uplifting Local Communities

In the realm of entrepreneurial metamorphosis, a powerful narrative emerges—one where entrepreneurs, driven by a sense of social responsibility and a commitment to positive impact, uplift local communities through their ventures. The subtopic "Uplifting Local Communities" delves into the stories of entrepreneurs who, cognizant of their roles as community stewards, leverage their ventures to bring about positive change, foster economic growth, and create lasting social impact. This chapter unveils narratives of community-centered entrepreneurship, illustrating the transformative power of businesses that prioritize the well-being and prosperity of the localities they serve.

The Ethos of Community-Centered Entrepreneurship

Community-centered entrepreneurship embodies a philosophy that transcends profit margins, placing equal emphasis on social impact and community well-being. Entrepreneurs within this theme share stories of how their ventures became agents of positive change, embracing an ethos that aligns business success with community upliftment.

The ethos of community-centered entrepreneurship involves a commitment to understanding the unique needs, challenges, and aspirations of local communities.

Entrepreneurs recount experiences of actively engaging with community members, conducting needs assessments, and co-creating solutions that contribute to the sustainable development of the areas they serve. The narratives become a guide for aspiring entrepreneurs, emphasizing the transformative potential of businesses that prioritize community welfare.

Local Economic Empowerment Through Job Creation

One of the primary ways entrepreneurs uplift local communities is through job creation. Entrepreneurs within this theme share stories of how their ventures became catalysts for local economic empowerment, providing employment opportunities, skills development, and economic stability to community members.

Job creation involves not only hiring individuals but also investing in their professional growth and well-being. Entrepreneurs recount experiences of implementing fair labor practices, offering training programs, and fostering inclusive workplaces that empower employees. The narratives become a testament to the transformative impact of businesses that prioritize local economic empowerment, illustrating that job creation goes beyond numbers to become a powerful force for community upliftment.

Supporting Local Supply Chains and Industries

Entrepreneurial ventures have the potential to breathe new life into local supply chains and industries, fostering economic resilience and sustainability. Entrepreneurs within this theme share stories of how their businesses actively supported local producers, artisans, and industries, creating a symbiotic relationship that uplifted the entire community.

Supporting local supply chains involves a deliberate choice to source materials locally, collaborate with local suppliers, and contribute to the growth of indigenous industries. Entrepreneurs recount experiences of building partnerships with local artisans, farmers, and manufacturers, ensuring fair compensation and fostering a sense of pride and ownership within the community. The narratives become a guide for entrepreneurs seeking to align their ventures with local economies, emphasizing the transformative potential of businesses that prioritize the sustainability of local supply chains.

Fostering Entrepreneurship Within Communities

Empowering local communities involves not only external support but also fostering a culture of entrepreneurship within the community itself. Entrepreneurs within this theme share stories of initiatives aimed at nurturing local talent, encouraging small-scale entrepreneurship, and creating an ecosystem where community members can transform their ideas into viable businesses.

Fostering entrepreneurship within communities involves providing mentorship, access to resources, and creating platforms for aspiring entrepreneurs to showcase their innovations. Entrepreneurs recount experiences of organizing entrepreneurship workshops, supporting local initiatives, and investing in programs that empower individuals to become entrepreneurs within their own communities. The narratives become a testament to the transformative power of businesses that actively contribute to the growth of an entrepreneurial culture, creating a ripple effect of positive change within communities.

Addressing Local Challenges Through Innovative Solutions

Local communities often face unique challenges that require innovative solutions. Entrepreneurs within this theme share stories of how their ventures identified pressing community issues and innovated solutions that not only addressed those challenges but also contributed to the overall well-being of the community.

Addressing local challenges involves a deep understanding of community needs, collaboration with local stakeholders, and a commitment to sustainable solutions. Entrepreneurs recount experiences of developing technologies, products, or services that directly addressed local challenges, whether in healthcare, education, environmental sustainability, or other areas. The narratives become a guide for entrepreneurs seeking to create meaningful impact, illustrating that businesses can be powerful vehicles for positive change when they align with the specific needs of the communities they serve.

Community Engagement and Collaboration

The success of community-centered entrepreneurship hinges on meaningful engagement and collaboration with local residents and organizations. Entrepreneurs within this theme share stories of how they actively engaged with the community, sought input from residents, and collaborated with local organizations to ensure that their ventures were aligned with community aspirations.

Community engagement involves creating spaces for dialogue, understanding cultural nuances, and building relationships based on trust and respect. Entrepreneurs recount experiences of collaborating with local NGOs, partnering with community leaders, and involving residents in decision-making processes. The narratives become a guide for entrepreneurs seeking to build businesses that are deeply rooted in the fabric of the communities they serve, illustrating that sustained impact requires active collaboration and genuine engagement.

Investing in Community Education and Skill Development

Entrepreneurial ventures have the power to be catalysts for education and skill development within local communities. Entrepreneurs within this theme share stories of initiatives aimed at improving educational opportunities, providing skill development programs, and contributing to the overall educational ecosystem of the community.

Investing in community education involves recognizing the importance of education as a driver of social mobility and economic empowerment. Entrepreneurs recount experiences of sponsoring local schools, organizing skill development workshops, and collaborating with educational institutions to enhance access to quality education. The narratives become a testament to the transformative impact of businesses that prioritize education and skill development as integral components of their community-centered approach.

Environmental Stewardship for Sustainable Communities

Entrepreneurial ventures that prioritize environmental stewardship contribute not only to global sustainability but also to the creation of healthier and more sustainable local communities. Entrepreneurs within this theme share stories of how their ventures embraced environmentally conscious practices, contributing to the well-being of the community and the planet.

Environmental stewardship involves adopting sustainable business practices, minimizing ecological impact, and actively contributing to environmental conservation efforts. Entrepreneurs recount experiences of implementing green initiatives, reducing carbon footprints, and engaging in community-led environmental projects. The narratives become a guide for entrepreneurs seeking to build businesses that are environmentally responsible and contribute to the creation of sustainable, resilient communities.

Measuring Social Impact and Creating Accountability

Entrepreneurial ventures committed to community upliftment often prioritize the measurement of social impact, ensuring transparency and accountability in their initiatives. Entrepreneurs within this theme share stories of implementing metrics, assessing social impact, and actively seeking feedback from the community to continuously improve their efforts.

Measuring social impact involves not only quantitative metrics but also qualitative assessments of the real-world changes experienced by community members. Entrepreneurs recount experiences of conducting impact assessments, collaborating with third-party evaluators, and using community feedback to refine and enhance their social impact initiatives. The narratives become a guide for entrepreneurs seeking to build businesses with a genuine commitment to social responsibility, illustrating that creating lasting change requires continuous evaluation and accountability.

Conclusion: The Ripple Effect of Community-Centered Entrepreneurship

In the chapter on "Uplifting Local Communities," the narratives of entrepreneurial metamorphosis converge to illuminate the transformative power of businesses that prioritize the well-being and prosperity of the communities they serve. As we immerse ourselves in the stories of entrepreneurs who actively uplifted local communities through job creation, sustainable practices, education initiatives, and innovative solutions, we witness not only the positive changes brought about within specific localities but also the ripple effect that community-centered entrepreneurship can have on the broader landscape of social and economic development. Each narrative becomes a testament to the enduring impact of businesses that recognize their role as community stewards, illustrating that true success in entrepreneurship is not just measured in financial terms but in the positive and lasting impact created within the communities that entrepreneurs call home.

Chapter 4: Second Chance Tales
Despair to Hope

In the tapestry of life, the thread of second chances weaves a narrative of resilience, redemption, and the transformative journey from despair to hope. The subtopic "Despair to Hope" in the chapter on Second Chance Tales explores the profound stories of individuals who, confronted with the depths of despair, found within themselves the strength to embark on a journey of renewal and optimism. This chapter delves into narratives of overcoming adversity, reclaiming one's sense of purpose, and discovering a newfound hope that serves as a beacon for others seeking their own second chances.

Navigating the Depths of Despair

Despair, with its suffocating weight, can be a profound force in an individual's life. The narratives within this theme unravel stories of individuals who found themselves in the darkest corners of despair—whether due to personal crises, societal challenges, or self-inflicted struggles. These stories offer a raw and honest exploration of the emotional and psychological toll that despair can exact on an individual, laying bare the vulnerabilities that often accompany moments of profound hopelessness.

The depths of despair are often marked by a sense of isolation, loss, and the erosion of one's sense of self. The narratives illustrate the myriad forms that despair can take—be it the aftermath of personal failures, the fallout from external circumstances, or the consequences of choices that led individuals down seemingly irreversible paths. Through these stories, we gain insights into the complex interplay of factors that contribute to despair and the varied ways in which individuals navigate this challenging terrain.

The Catalysts for Change

Amidst the darkness of despair, a common thread emerges—the catalysts for change that become pivotal in shifting the trajectory from hopelessness to the possibility of a second chance. These catalysts take diverse forms, ranging from moments of profound introspection and external interventions to the serendipitous encounters that can alter the course of an individual's life.

The narratives delve into the catalysts that served as turning points, prompting individuals to confront their despair and take the first steps toward transformation. Whether it's a moment of self-realization, the support of a mentor or loved one, or an unexpected opportunity that opens a door to change, these catalysts become beacons of hope, guiding individuals out of the depths of despair and towards the possibility of a brighter future.

The Journey of Self-Rediscovery

Central to the narrative of despair to hope is the journey of self-rediscovery—an exploration of identity, values, and purpose that becomes a compass for those seeking a second chance. The narratives within this theme unravel stories of individuals who embarked on profound journeys of introspection, peeling away the layers of despair to uncover the core of their authentic selves.

The journey of self-rediscovery often involves confronting past traumas, reassessing personal beliefs, and redefining one's sense of purpose. These narratives become windows into the transformative power of self-reflection and the courageous pursuit of personal growth. Through the stories of self-rediscovery, we witness individuals reclaiming agency over their lives and forging a path towards hope and renewal.

Overcoming Personal Demons

Despair is often intertwined with personal demons—internal struggles, addictions, or destructive patterns of behavior that exacerbate feelings of hopelessness. The narratives within this theme illuminate stories of individuals who confronted and overcame their personal demons, breaking free from the shackles of self-destructive behaviors that fueled their despair.

Overcoming personal demons requires a profound commitment to self-healing and a willingness to seek help when needed. The narratives share the varied paths individuals took—whether through therapy, support groups, or other forms of intervention—to overcome the challenges that perpetuated their despair. These stories become testaments to the resilience of the human spirit and the transformative potential of confronting and conquering one's inner demons.

Seeking Redemption and Forgiveness

The journey from despair to hope often involves seeking redemption and forgiveness, both from oneself and from those who may have been affected by past actions. The narratives within this theme unravel stories of individuals grappling with guilt, remorse, and the arduous process of rebuilding trust and relationships that may have been fractured in the depths of despair.

Redemption and forgiveness are not easy paths, and the narratives offer a nuanced exploration of the complexities involved. Individuals share experiences of atonement, making amends, and the transformative power of forgiveness—both receiving and extending it. Through these stories, we gain insights into the cathartic nature of seeking redemption and the profound impact it can have on one's journey towards hope and renewal.

Embracing Second Chances

The essence of the despair-to-hope narrative lies in the embrace of second chances—the recognition that, despite past mistakes or circumstances, individuals possess the agency to rewrite their stories. The narratives within this theme unfold stories of individuals who, having confronted their despair and undergone profound transformations, embraced the opportunity for a second chance.

Embracing second chances involves a commitment to change, resilience in the face of setbacks, and a hopeful outlook towards the future. These stories become beacons for others who may find themselves in the depths of despair, illustrating that the journey towards hope begins with a willingness to believe in the possibility of a new beginning.

Paying It Forward: Becoming Agents of Change

The transformative journey from despair to hope often instills in individuals a deep sense of empathy and a desire to make a positive impact on others. The narratives within this theme unravel stories of individuals who, having navigated their own despair, became agents of change in their communities, paying forward the support and opportunities that contributed to their own second chances.

Paying it forward involves a commitment to creating positive ripples in the lives of others—whether through mentorship, advocacy, or initiatives that address the root causes of despair. These stories become testaments to the transformative power of compassion and the profound impact individuals can have when they choose to use their experiences to uplift others.

Conclusion: Illuminating the Path from Despair to Hope

In the chapter on "Second Chance Tales," the narratives converge to illuminate the transformative journey from the depths of despair to the radiant light of hope. As we immerse ourselves in the stories of individuals who confronted their despair, found catalysts for change, embarked on journeys of self-rediscovery, and embraced second chances, we witness not only personal transformations but also the enduring ripple effects that extend to others. Each narrative becomes a testament to the resilience of the human spirit, illustrating that even in the darkest moments, there exists the potential for renewal, redemption, and the embrace of a hopeful future.

Redemption and Forgiveness

In the intricate tapestry of second chances, the threads of redemption and forgiveness intertwine, weaving a narrative of healing, growth, and the transformative power of reconciliation. The subtopic "Redemption and Forgiveness" in the chapter on Second Chance Tales explores the profound stories of individuals who, having traversed the shadows of despair, sought redemption for their past actions and grappled with the complex journey of forgiveness. This chapter delves into narratives of atonement, the restoration of relationships, and the cathartic release that comes with both seeking and extending forgiveness.

Confronting the Shadows: The Need for Redemption

Redemption, as a theme within the narratives of second chances, is a process that involves acknowledging and atoning for past mistakes, actions, or decisions that may have contributed to one's descent into despair. The narratives within this theme unravel stories of individuals who confronted the shadows of their own actions, took accountability for the consequences, and embarked on the path of redemption.

The need for redemption often arises from a deep sense of remorse and the desire to make amends. Individuals share experiences of reflecting on the impact of their actions, recognizing the harm caused to themselves and others, and the inner imperative to seek redemption as a step toward personal and moral restoration. Through these stories, we explore the complexities of redemption, understanding that it is not a singular act but a transformative journey of self-discovery and growth.

Atonement and Making Amends

Central to the theme of redemption is the notion of atonement—the deliberate effort to make amends for past wrongs. The narratives within this theme unfold stories of individuals who, having acknowledged their mistakes, took proactive steps to address the repercussions and repair the fabric of relationships and communities torn by their actions.

Atonement involves actions that go beyond words, signaling a genuine commitment to change. Individuals share experiences of restitution, community service, and tangible efforts to rectify the harm caused. These stories become testaments to the transformative power of atonement, illustrating that the journey toward redemption requires not only internal reflection but external actions that align with the values of accountability and responsibility.

The Complex Landscape of Forgiveness

Forgiveness, a counterpoint to redemption, introduces a nuanced and complex landscape within the narratives of second chances. The stories within this theme navigate the intricate dynamics of forgiveness—both seeking it for oneself and extending it to others. Forgiveness, as a theme, invites exploration into the emotional, psychological, and spiritual dimensions of releasing resentment and embracing healing.

Forgiveness is not a linear process, and the narratives unfold stories of individuals grappling with the complexities of forgiving oneself and, equally challenging, forgiving others. These stories reveal the internal conflicts, the emotional upheavals, and the gradual, often non-linear journey toward forgiveness. The exploration of forgiveness becomes a profound examination of the human capacity to transcend pain and find solace in the act of letting go.

Rebuilding Trust: The Fragile Architecture of Redemption

Redemption, while often an internal and personal journey, intersects with the external realm of relationships and trust. The narratives within this theme delve into the delicate process of rebuilding trust—both with oneself and with those who may have been affected by past actions. Rebuilding trust becomes an integral aspect of the redemption narrative, requiring patience, consistency, and a commitment to sustained change.

The stories unfold experiences of individuals navigating the fragility of trust, recognizing that rebuilding is a gradual process that demands transparency, reliability, and a demonstrated shift in behavior. The narratives become a guide for others who may be on the path of redemption, illustrating that the restoration of trust is not just about words but about consistent actions that align with the values of growth and transformation.

The Cathartic Release of Forgiveness

Forgiveness, when sought and granted, becomes a cathartic release—a transformative act that liberates individuals from the shackles of resentment, anger, and bitterness. The narratives within this theme share stories of the profound emotional and psychological impact of forgiveness, both for the individuals seeking redemption and for those extending the gift of forgiveness.

The cathartic release of forgiveness is depicted as a moment of profound healing, offering individuals the opportunity to break free from the emotional burdens that may have accompanied their journey through despair. The stories illuminate the transformative power of forgiveness in fostering inner peace, emotional well-being, and the restoration of a positive outlook on life. Through these narratives, we witness the ripple effects of forgiveness, transcending the immediate parties involved and extending to broader communities.

Navigating the Roadblocks to Forgiveness

The journey toward forgiveness is not without roadblocks, and the narratives within this theme confront the challenges and complexities that individuals face in their quest for forgiveness. These roadblocks may include resistance to letting go of anger, the fear of vulnerability, or the struggle to reconcile conflicting emotions.

Individuals share experiences of navigating these roadblocks, employing strategies such as therapy, support groups, and spiritual practices to overcome the barriers to forgiveness. The narratives become a source of insight for others on a similar journey, offering perspectives on resilience and perseverance in the face of the challenges that may accompany the pursuit of forgiveness.

The Transformative Power of Compassion

Compassion emerges as a recurring theme within the narratives of redemption and forgiveness. The stories within this theme unfold instances where individuals, having experienced the transformative power of compassion from others or having cultivated it within themselves, extended compassion to those who may have wronged them.

Compassion becomes a guiding force in the forgiveness narrative, illustrating that the ability to empathize with the struggles and mistakes of others can be a catalyst for healing and reconciliation. The narratives become beacons of compassion, illustrating that forgiveness is not only a personal journey but also a collective and reciprocal act that has the potential to mend the fabric of relationships and communities.

The Ripple Effects of Redemption and Forgiveness

In the chapter on "Redemption and Forgiveness," the narratives of second chances converge to illuminate the transformative power of seeking redemption and extending forgiveness. As we immerse ourselves in the stories of individuals who confronted the shadows of their past, sought atonement, and navigated the intricate landscape of forgiveness, we witness not only personal transformations but also the profound impact on relationships, communities, and the broader fabric of human connection. Each narrative becomes a testament to the resilience of the human spirit, illustrating that the journey toward redemption and forgiveness is not just an individual pursuit but a collective effort to heal, grow, and create a more compassionate and understanding world.

Valuable Perspectives Gained

In the mosaic of second chances, the subtopic "Valuable Perspectives Gained" unveils stories of profound personal transformation, where individuals, having navigated the tumultuous terrain of despair and redemption, emerge with a heightened awareness and invaluable insights. This chapter explores narratives that delve into the perspectives gained through the journey of second chances—perspectives that encompass self-discovery, empathy, resilience, and a profound appreciation for the intricate tapestry of human experience.

A Shift in Perception: Seeing Beyond the Surface

The narratives within this theme unravel stories of individuals whose journey from despair to hope prompted a fundamental shift in their perception of themselves and the world around them. Whether through introspection, external support, or transformative experiences, these individuals share how they began to see beyond the surface of their circumstances and gained a deeper understanding of the complexities that shape human lives.

A shift in perception involves recognizing the nuances of one's own story and the stories of others. The narratives become a testament to the transformative power of gaining a broader perspective, illustrating that valuable insights often emerge when individuals transcend surface-level judgments and embrace a more compassionate and nuanced view of the world.

Cultivating Empathy Through Shared Struggles

One of the invaluable perspectives gained through the journey of second chances is the cultivation of empathy. The narratives within this theme unfold stories of individuals who, having faced their own struggles, developed a heightened sense of empathy for the challenges faced by others. These stories illustrate how personal experiences of despair and redemption became catalysts for a more compassionate understanding of the human condition.

Cultivating empathy involves not only recognizing the shared aspects of the human experience but also actively seeking to understand and relate to the struggles of others. The narratives become a source of inspiration for individuals on similar journeys, emphasizing that the empathy gained through personal trials has the potential to foster connection, dismantle judgment, and contribute to the creation of a more empathetic and supportive society.

Resilience as a Source of Strength

Resilience emerges as a recurring theme within the narratives of valuable perspectives gained. Individuals share stories of navigating the challenges of despair, confronting personal demons, and rebuilding their lives, illustrating the transformative power of resilience as a source of strength.

Resilience involves not only bouncing back from adversity but also adapting, growing, and thriving in the face of challenges. The narratives become a guide for others seeking to cultivate resilience, offering insights into the mindset shifts, coping mechanisms, and personal growth that contribute to the development of resilience. These stories become beacons of hope, affirming that resilience is not just a trait but a dynamic and evolving process that can be harnessed to navigate the complexities of life.

The Beauty of Imperfection: Embracing Flaws and Failures

The journey from despair to hope often involves a profound shift in perspective regarding imperfections, flaws, and failures. The narratives within this theme unfold stories of individuals who, having confronted their own imperfections and failures, gained a deeper appreciation for the beauty inherent in the imperfect nature of the human experience.

Embracing flaws and failures involves dismantling the unrealistic expectations of perfection and recognizing the inherent value in the journey of growth and self-discovery. The narratives become a celebration of authenticity, illustrating that the acceptance of imperfections is not a sign of weakness but a testament to the resilience and courage required to confront and overcome personal challenges.

An Altered Relationship with Time: The Present Moment and Future Possibilities

The transformative journey of second chances often brings about an altered relationship with time—an increased appreciation for the present moment and a hopeful gaze toward future possibilities. Individuals share stories of how their experiences of despair and redemption prompted a reevaluation of their relationship with time, emphasizing the importance of living in the present and embracing the potential for positive change in the future.

An altered relationship with time involves a shift away from dwelling on past mistakes or anxieties about the future and a focus on the opportunities and experiences available in the present moment. The narratives become a call to action for individuals to seize the opportunities for growth, connection, and joy that exist in the now, while maintaining a hopeful outlook toward the possibilities that lie ahead.

The Intersection of Humility and Gratitude

Humility and gratitude emerge as intertwined themes within the narratives of valuable perspectives gained. Individuals share stories of how their journey through despair humbled them, breaking down ego-driven barriers and fostering a profound sense of gratitude for the opportunities, relationships, and second chances that life presented.

Humility involves a recognition of one's own vulnerabilities and a willingness to learn from both successes and failures. Gratitude, in turn, becomes a natural outgrowth of humility, as individuals express appreciation for the supportive networks, transformative experiences, and moments of grace that contributed to their journey of second chances. The narratives become a testament to the transformative power of cultivating humility and gratitude as integral components of a meaningful and purposeful life.

Shifting Priorities: What Truly Matters in Life

The narratives within this theme unveil stories of individuals who, having traversed the landscape of despair and redemption, experienced a shift in priorities—a reevaluation of what truly matters in life. These stories illustrate how the journey of second chances prompted individuals to move beyond superficial pursuits and focus on the intrinsic values that bring meaning and fulfillment.

Shifting priorities involves aligning one's actions, goals, and aspirations with a deeper understanding of personal values, relationships, and the pursuit of genuine happiness. The narratives become a guide for individuals seeking to recalibrate their priorities, emphasizing that the journey of second chances often leads to a more intentional and purposeful way of living.

A Commitment to Lifelong Learning and Growth

The journey from despair to hope is an ongoing process of learning and growth, and the narratives within this theme underscore the commitment of individuals to continuous self-improvement. These stories illustrate how the valuable perspectives gained through the journey of second chances become a foundation for a lifelong commitment to learning, adapting, and evolving.

A commitment to lifelong learning involves a recognition that personal growth is a dynamic and ever-evolving process. The narratives become a source of inspiration for individuals on similar journeys, highlighting the transformative potential of embracing a mindset of curiosity, resilience, and a dedication to becoming the best versions of themselves.

Conclusion: Illuminating the Tapestry of Human Experience

In the chapter on "Valuable Perspectives Gained," the narratives of second chances converge to illuminate the intricate tapestry of human experience. As we immerse ourselves in the stories of individuals who gained valuable perspectives through their journey from despair to hope, we witness not only personal transformations but also the universal themes that connect us all. Each narrative becomes a testament to the resilience of the human spirit and the profound insights that can emerge from the crucible of despair, illustrating that the journey of second chances is not just a personal quest but a collective exploration of the complexities, beauty, and shared humanity that define the human experience.

Making Amends Through Service

In the symphony of second chances, the subtopic "Making Amends Through Service" unveils narratives of individuals who, having traversed the shadows of despair and sought redemption, discovered a profound avenue for transformation—service to others. This chapter explores stories of individuals who, recognizing the impact of their past actions, embarked on a journey of making amends through dedicated service to their communities, fostering a sense of purpose, connection, and positive change.

Recognizing the Impact: A Catalyst for Service

The narratives within this theme unravel stories of individuals who, through introspection and self-awareness, came to recognize the impact of their past actions on themselves and those around them. This recognition served as a catalyst for a transformative shift—one that prompted individuals to move beyond remorse and actively seek ways to make amends.

Recognizing the impact involves a deep and honest reflection on the consequences of one's actions, acknowledging the harm caused, and understanding the potential for positive change. The narratives become a testament to the power of self-awareness as a precursor to meaningful service, illustrating that the journey of making amends begins with a genuine understanding of the impact of past behavior.

Service as a Path to Redemption

The narratives within this theme unfold stories of individuals who, driven by a desire for redemption, found solace and purpose in service to others. Service became a path to redemption—an active and tangible way for individuals to demonstrate their commitment to positive change and to contribute to the well-being of their communities.

Service as a path to redemption involves actions that go beyond words, offering individuals the opportunity to actively participate in the healing and growth of those they may have impacted. The narratives become a guide for others on similar journeys, emphasizing that service is not only a means of making amends but also a transformative journey of self-discovery, empathy, and community connection.

Community Connection: From Isolation to Contribution

The journey of making amends through service often involves a shift from isolation to active contribution within the community. The narratives within this theme share stories of individuals who, having experienced the isolating effects of despair, discovered a renewed sense of purpose and belonging through service.

Community connection involves recognizing one's place within the broader social fabric and actively engaging with the community to foster positive change. The narratives become a testament to the transformative power of community involvement, illustrating that service not only benefits others but also becomes a source of personal fulfillment, connection, and the rebuilding of social bonds.

Addressing Root Causes: Beyond Surface-Level Impact

The narratives within this theme delve into stories of individuals who, in their journey of making amends through service, sought to address the root causes of the issues they may have contributed to in the past. Whether tackling issues related to addiction, poverty, or social injustice, these individuals became advocates for systemic change, recognizing that addressing surface-level symptoms is insufficient for meaningful impact.

Addressing root causes involves a commitment to understanding the underlying factors that contribute to social challenges and actively working towards systemic solutions. The narratives become a source of inspiration for individuals seeking to make amends in a way that goes beyond surface-level impact, emphasizing the importance of tackling the root causes to create lasting positive change.

From Recipient to Giver: The Transformative Power of Service

The narratives within this theme illuminate stories of individuals who, having once been recipients of support or assistance, experienced a transformative shift by becoming givers through service. This shift—from being a recipient to a giver—became a powerful aspect of their journey of making amends, fostering a sense of agency, empowerment, and reciprocity.

From recipient to giver involves a shift in mindset—from a position of dependence to one of active contribution. The narratives become a testament to the reciprocal nature of service, illustrating that the act of giving not only benefits the recipients but also becomes a source of personal empowerment and fulfillment for those making amends through service.

Educational Initiatives: Empowering Through Knowledge

The narratives within this theme unfold stories of individuals who, in their commitment to making amends, became advocates for educational initiatives as a means of empowerment. Recognizing the transformative power of knowledge, these individuals engaged in initiatives that aimed to uplift and educate others, particularly those who may have been affected by their past actions.

Educational initiatives involve a commitment to providing access to information, resources, and opportunities for personal and collective growth. The narratives become a source of inspiration for individuals seeking to make amends through education, emphasizing that empowering others through knowledge is a powerful pathway to positive change.

Social Entrepreneurship: Building Sustainable Solutions

The journey of making amends through service often intersects with stories of social entrepreneurship—individuals who, having recognized the impact of their past actions, became pioneers of sustainable solutions to address societal challenges. These narratives share stories of individuals who, through innovative and socially conscious business ventures, sought to create positive and lasting change.

Social entrepreneurship involves a commitment to addressing social, environmental, or economic issues through entrepreneurial ventures that prioritize both profit and positive impact. The narratives become a guide for individuals seeking to make amends through sustainable solutions, illustrating that entrepreneurship can be a powerful vehicle for creating meaningful and lasting change.

Restorative Justice: Transforming Harm into Healing

Restorative justice emerges as a theme within the narratives of making amends through service, offering a transformative approach to addressing harm and fostering healing. The stories within this theme illustrate how individuals, having recognized the impact of their actions, actively engaged in restorative justice initiatives to repair harm and rebuild relationships.

Restorative justice involves a process of acknowledging responsibility, making amends to those who have been harmed, and actively participating in the healing of affected individuals and communities. The narratives become a testament to the potential of restorative justice as a powerful and transformative tool for individuals seeking to make amends and contribute to the restoration of social harmony.

Conclusion: The Transformative Impact of Service

In the chapter on "Making Amends Through Service," the narratives of second chances converge to illuminate the transformative impact of service on individuals, communities, and the broader fabric of society. As we immerse ourselves in the stories of individuals who, having recognized the impact of their past actions, actively engaged in service to make amends, we witness not only personal transformations but also the profound ripple effects that extend to the well-being of others. Each narrative becomes a testament to the resilience of the human spirit and the redemptive power of service as a catalyst for positive change.

Chapter 5: Wellness Transformation Journeys
Health Crises

In the labyrinth of wellness transformation journeys, the subtopic "Health Crises" unravels narratives of individuals whose lives took an unexpected turn, marked by profound health challenges. This chapter explores stories of resilience, self-discovery, and transformation as individuals confront health crises head-on, navigating the complexities of physical and mental well-being. Through these narratives, we gain insights into the transformative power of facing health crises, the strength found in vulnerability, and the journey toward holistic wellness.

The Unforeseen Journey: Confronting Health Crises

The narratives within this theme share stories of individuals who, once on a different path, were suddenly thrust into the uncharted territory of health crises. Whether facing chronic illnesses, sudden injuries, or life-altering diagnoses, these individuals found themselves grappling with the fragility of their physical and mental well-being.

Confronting health crises involves navigating the shock, uncertainty, and emotional upheaval that often accompany unexpected health challenges. The narratives become windows into the raw and unfiltered experiences of individuals who, in the face of adversity, discovered reservoirs of strength, resilience, and a determination to navigate the unforeseen journey toward wellness.

The Emotional Landscape of Health Crises

Health crises extend beyond the physical realm, delving into the emotional landscape where individuals navigate fear, grief, and the profound impact of uncertainty. The stories within this theme unravel the emotional rollercoaster experienced by individuals facing health challenges, shedding light on the psychological toll that accompanies the physical aspects of illness.

The emotional landscape of health crises involves grappling with the fear of the unknown, mourning the loss of normalcy, and confronting existential questions about life and mortality. The narratives become a testament to the importance of addressing the holistic well-being of individuals facing health crises, acknowledging the interconnectedness of physical and mental health in the journey toward recovery and transformation.

The Quest for Understanding: Navigating Diagnoses and Treatments

In the midst of health crises, individuals often embark on a quest for understanding—a journey that involves seeking clarity about diagnoses, exploring treatment options, and navigating the intricacies of the healthcare system. The narratives within this theme unfold stories of individuals who became advocates for their own health, engaged in informed decision-making, and sought partnerships with healthcare professionals to navigate the complexities of their medical journeys.

The quest for understanding involves not only gaining knowledge about medical conditions and treatment options but also advocating for personalized and patient-centered care. The narratives become a guide for others facing health crises, emphasizing the importance of empowerment, collaboration, and a proactive approach in the pursuit of wellness.

The Support Ecosystem: Nurturing Connection Amidst Crisis

Health crises often illuminate the significance of a robust support ecosystem—a network of relationships, both professional and personal, that plays a vital role in the healing journey. The narratives within this theme share stories of individuals who, facing health challenges, found solace, strength, and resilience in the connections forged with healthcare professionals, family members, friends, and support groups.

The support ecosystem involves not only the provision of medical care but also emotional support, empathy, and a sense of belonging. The narratives become a testament to the transformative power of nurturing connections amidst crisis, illustrating that the collective strength of a support network can be a cornerstone in the journey toward wellness and recovery.

Navigating Treatment Trajectories: Balancing Hope and Realism

The journey through health crises often involves navigating treatment trajectories—a delicate balance between holding onto hope and confronting the realities of medical interventions. The narratives within this theme unfold stories of individuals who, facing various treatment options, made decisions that aligned with their values, goals, and aspirations.

Navigating treatment trajectories involves grappling with the complexities of medical choices, potential side effects, and the emotional toll of decision-making. The narratives become a guide for others on similar journeys, offering insights into the importance of informed decision-making, clear communication with healthcare providers, and the ongoing evaluation and adjustment of treatment plans in the pursuit of wellness.

Chronic Illness Narratives: Embracing Life Amidst Limitations

For individuals facing chronic illnesses, the narrative of wellness transformation becomes an ongoing journey of embracing life amidst limitations. The stories within this theme share experiences of individuals who, despite the enduring nature of their health challenges, discovered resilience, purpose, and a redefined sense of normalcy.

Chronic illness narratives involve not only the management of symptoms and medical interventions but also the cultivation of a positive mindset, adaptive strategies, and a focus on the aspects of life that bring joy and fulfillment. The narratives become beacons for others navigating chronic illnesses, illustrating that wellness transformation is not always about cure but about finding meaning and joy in the journey.

Mental Health Challenges: Breaking Stigmas, Seeking Support

The narratives within this theme unfold stories of individuals confronting mental health challenges—navigating the intricacies of diagnoses, treatments, and the societal stigmas that often surround mental health. These stories become a powerful exploration of the transformative journey toward mental well-being, emphasizing the importance of breaking stigmas, seeking support, and fostering a holistic approach to mental health care.

Mental health challenges involve not only the management of symptoms but also the destigmatization of mental health issues and the promotion of open conversations. The narratives become a call to action for individuals facing mental health challenges, urging them to seek support, prioritize self-care, and contribute to the collective effort to dismantle barriers to mental well-being.

The Role of Lifestyle Changes: Holistic Approaches to Wellness

In the face of health crises, individuals often discover the transformative potential of lifestyle changes—adopting holistic approaches to wellness that encompass not only medical interventions but also changes in diet, exercise, stress management, and overall lifestyle. The narratives within this theme share stories of individuals who, recognizing the interconnectedness of physical and mental health, embraced lifestyle changes as integral components of their wellness transformation journeys.

Lifestyle changes involve a commitment to cultivating habits that promote overall well-being, resilience, and a sense of balance. The narratives become a source of inspiration for individuals seeking to integrate holistic approaches to wellness, illustrating that transformative change often extends beyond medical treatments to encompass the choices individuals make in their daily lives.

The Journey Toward Acceptance: Redefining Wellness

Amidst health crises, individuals often embark on a journey toward acceptance—a process that involves coming to terms with the realities of their health conditions, embracing resilience, and redefining the meaning of wellness. The narratives within this theme share stories of individuals who, having confronted the challenges of their health journeys, found a sense of peace, purpose, and a redefined understanding of what it means to be well.

The journey toward acceptance involves acknowledging limitations, cultivating self-compassion, and focusing on aspects of life that contribute to a sense of fulfillment and joy. The narratives become guides for others on similar journeys, emphasizing that wellness transformation is a dynamic process that involves not only physical health but also the nurturing of emotional, social, and spiritual well-being.

Conclusion: Illuminating the Path to Holistic Wellness

In the chapter on "Wellness Transformation Journeys," the narratives of individuals facing health crises converge to illuminate the path to holistic wellness. As we immerse ourselves in the stories of resilience, self-discovery, and transformation, we witness not only the challenges of health crises but also the profound capacity for individuals to navigate adversity and redefine what it means to be well. Each narrative becomes a testament to the resilience of the human spirit and the transformative power of confronting health crises as a catalyst for holistic wellness.

Commitment to Healing

In the odyssey of wellness transformation journeys, the subtopic "Commitment to Healing" delves into narratives of individuals who, faced with the labyrinth of health challenges, embarked on a steadfast journey toward recovery, resilience, and holistic well-being. This chapter explores stories of unwavering commitment—individuals who, in the face of adversity, embraced healing as a multifaceted and ongoing process, transcending the confines of physical ailments to nurture their mental, emotional, and spiritual well-being.

Initiating the Healing Journey: Acknowledging the Need for Change

The narratives within this theme reveal stories of individuals who, confronted with health challenges, took the pivotal step of acknowledging the need for change. This acknowledgment marked the initiation of their healing journey—an awareness that prompted a commitment to addressing not only the symptoms of their conditions but also the underlying factors contributing to their well-being.

Initiating the healing journey involves a profound self-reflection, an acknowledgment of vulnerabilities, and a commitment to take proactive steps toward recovery. The narratives become a testament to the transformative power of recognizing the need for change, illustrating that healing begins with a conscious decision to embark on a journey of self-discovery and well-being.

Holistic Perspectives: Beyond Symptomatic Treatment

The narratives within this theme unfold stories of individuals who, in their commitment to healing, embraced holistic perspectives—approaches that transcend symptomatic treatment to address the interconnected aspects of their physical, mental, and emotional well-being. These individuals recognized that true healing involves not only alleviating symptoms but also nurturing a balanced and integrated approach to health.

Holistic perspectives involve an understanding of the interplay between physical, mental, and emotional factors in the healing process. The narratives become a guide for others seeking a holistic approach to well-being, emphasizing the importance of considering the broader context of health and embracing modalities that contribute to the overall harmony of mind, body, and spirit.

Patient Advocacy: Empowering Individuals in Their Healing Journey

The journey toward healing often intersects with patient advocacy—individuals actively participating in their healthcare decisions, seeking information, and advocating for their well-being. The narratives within this theme share stories of individuals who became advocates for themselves, collaborating with healthcare professionals, and actively engaging in decisions that aligned with their values and goals.

Patient advocacy involves empowerment, informed decision-making, and fostering a collaborative relationship with healthcare providers. The narratives become a source of inspiration for individuals navigating health challenges, illustrating that a commitment to healing includes active engagement, self-advocacy, and a partnership with healthcare professionals in the pursuit of well-being.

Cultivating Resilience: Navigating Setbacks in the Healing Process

The healing journey is often marked by setbacks—moments of uncertainty, challenges, and unforeseen obstacles that individuals must navigate. The narratives within this theme unfold stories of resilience—individuals who, despite facing setbacks, remained steadfast in their commitment to healing, learning, and growing through the adversities encountered on their path.

Cultivating resilience involves developing the inner strength to navigate challenges, bounce back from setbacks, and adapt to the evolving nature of the healing process. The narratives become a guide for others on similar journeys, emphasizing that resilience is not the absence of challenges but the ability to respond to them with courage, perseverance, and a commitment to continued growth.

Mind-Body Connection: Harnessing the Power of Positive Thought

The narratives within this theme share stories of individuals who, in their commitment to healing, harnessed the power of the mind-body connection—recognizing that positive thought and mental well-being play integral roles in the overall healing process. These individuals embraced practices that fostered a positive mindset, resilience, and a sense of agency in their journey toward well-being.

The mind-body connection involves understanding the reciprocal relationship between mental and physical health, acknowledging the impact of thoughts and emotions on the healing process. The narratives become a source of inspiration for individuals seeking to harness the power of positive thought, emphasizing that cultivating a positive mindset can contribute significantly to the overall well-being and healing journey.

Complementary Therapies: Integrating Alternative Approaches

The commitment to healing often involves an openness to complementary therapies—alternative approaches that complement conventional medical treatments and contribute to the overall well-being of individuals facing health challenges. The narratives within this theme share stories of individuals who, in their commitment to healing, explored and integrated complementary therapies such as acupuncture, meditation, yoga, and other holistic modalities.

Complementary therapies involve a recognition that healing is multifaceted, encompassing physical, mental, and spiritual dimensions. The narratives become a guide for individuals seeking to explore alternative approaches, illustrating that the integration of complementary therapies can enhance the overall healing experience and contribute to a more comprehensive sense of well-being.

Embracing Lifestyle Changes: Sustainable Well-Being Practices

The commitment to healing often extends to embracing lifestyle changes—adopting practices that foster sustainable well-being and contribute to the long-term health of individuals. The narratives within this theme unfold stories of individuals who, recognizing the impact of lifestyle choices on their health, made intentional changes in areas such as diet, exercise, stress management, and sleep to support their healing journey.

Embracing lifestyle changes involves a commitment to cultivating habits that promote overall well-being and resilience. The narratives become a source of inspiration for individuals seeking to make sustainable changes in their lives, emphasizing that small, intentional shifts in lifestyle can have profound and lasting effects on the healing journey.

Spiritual Exploration: Finding Meaning and Connection

The narratives within this theme share stories of individuals who, in their commitment to healing, engaged in spiritual exploration—seeking meaning, connection, and a sense of purpose beyond the physical aspects of their health. These individuals discovered that spiritual practices, whether rooted in religious traditions or personal beliefs, played a transformative role in their healing journey.

Spiritual exploration involves a connection to a sense of purpose, a deeper understanding of the self, and a recognition of the interconnectedness of all aspects of life. The narratives become a guide for individuals seeking to integrate spiritual practices into their healing journey, illustrating that finding meaning and connection can be a powerful source of resilience and well-being.

Social Support: The Healing Power of Connection

The commitment to healing often unfolds within the context of social support—nurturing connections with family, friends, support groups, and the broader community. The narratives within this theme share stories of individuals who, surrounded by a network of supportive relationships, found solace, encouragement, and a sense of belonging in their healing journey.

Social support involves recognizing the importance of connection, empathy, and understanding in the healing process. The narratives become a testament to the healing power of relationships, emphasizing that the journey toward well-being is often enriched by the presence of a supportive community that encourages and uplifts individuals facing health challenges.

Self-Reflection and Mindfulness: Cultivating Present-Moment Awareness

The narratives within this theme reveal stories of individuals who, in their commitment to healing, embraced self-reflection and mindfulness—cultivating present-moment awareness as a means of navigating the complexities of their health challenges. These individuals discovered that the practice of mindfulness contributed to a deeper understanding of themselves, enhanced resilience, and a sense of peace in the midst of uncertainty.

Self-reflection and mindfulness involve cultivating an awareness of thoughts, emotions, and experiences in the present moment. The narratives become a guide for individuals seeking to integrate mindfulness into their healing journey, illustrating that the practice of present-moment awareness can foster resilience, reduce stress, and enhance overall well-being.

Conclusion: The Ever-Unfolding Journey of Healing

In the chapter on "Wellness Transformation Journeys," the narratives of commitment to healing converge to illuminate the ever-unfolding nature of the healing journey. As we immerse ourselves in the stories of individuals who, faced with health challenges, committed to holistic well-being, we witness not only the complexities of healing but also the profound capacity for individuals to actively participate in their own transformative journey. Each narrative becomes a testament to the resilience of the human spirit and the transformative power of a steadfast commitment to healing as a multifaceted and ongoing process.

Funding Research

In the intricate tapestry of wellness transformation journeys, the subtopic "Funding Research" unveils narratives of individuals who, propelled by their own health challenges, dedicated themselves to advancing medical knowledge, pushing the boundaries of scientific understanding, and actively contributing to the funding of research initiatives. This chapter explores stories of resilience, innovation, and the transformative power of leveraging personal experiences to drive impactful change in the realm of healthcare and medical research.

A Personal Catalyst for Change: Turning Adversity into Advocacy

The narratives within this theme share stories of individuals who, faced with their own health challenges or those of their loved ones, transformed adversity into advocacy. Motivated by a desire to create meaningful change, these individuals became catalysts for progress by channeling their personal experiences into a commitment to fund and advance medical research.

A personal catalyst for change involves a profound shift—from being a passive recipient of medical care to becoming an active advocate for progress in the field. The narratives become a testament to the transformative power of turning adversity into advocacy, illustrating that personal challenges can serve as powerful motivators for individuals to contribute to the broader landscape of medical knowledge.

Philanthropy in Health: A Commitment to Advancing Knowledge

The narratives within this theme unfold stories of individuals who, recognizing the critical role of philanthropy in advancing healthcare, made a commitment to fund research initiatives. These individuals understood that supporting medical research goes beyond personal benefits—it is a way to contribute to the collective well-being of society, drive scientific innovation, and create a lasting impact on future generations.

Philanthropy in health involves a conscious decision to allocate resources towards initiatives that have the potential to transform the landscape of healthcare and medical research. The narratives become a guide for others seeking to make a meaningful impact, emphasizing that philanthropy is not just a financial contribution but a commitment to the advancement of knowledge and the improvement of healthcare outcomes.

Patient-Led Research Initiatives: Bridging Gaps in Understanding

In the commitment to funding research, some individuals took the initiative further by actively participating in or leading research endeavors related to their health conditions. The narratives within this theme share stories of patient-led research initiatives—individuals who, driven by a desire for deeper understanding and improved outcomes, actively engaged in research activities to bridge gaps in medical knowledge.

Patient-led research initiatives involve a collaboration between individuals with lived experiences and the scientific community, fostering a more comprehensive understanding of health conditions. The narratives become a source of inspiration for individuals seeking to actively contribute to research, emphasizing the unique insights that patients can bring to the scientific community and the potential for collaborative efforts to drive transformative change.

Building Research Foundations: Establishing Endowments and Foundations

Some narratives within this theme unfold stories of individuals who, in their commitment to funding research, went beyond individual contributions to establish endowments and foundations. These entities serve as enduring legacies, providing sustained support for medical research initiatives and creating a framework for long-term impact.

Building research foundations involves a strategic and sustainable approach to philanthropy, with a focus on establishing structures that can support ongoing research efforts. The narratives become a guide for those considering a lasting impact in the field of medical research, illustrating the potential for individuals to create enduring contributions that outlive their individual lifetimes.

Collaboration with Research Institutions: A Partnership for Progress

The commitment to funding research often involves collaborations with research institutions—forging partnerships that leverage both financial support and the expertise of scientific communities. The narratives within this theme share stories of individuals who, recognizing the importance of collaboration, actively engaged with research institutions to amplify the impact of their contributions.

Collaboration with research institutions involves a dynamic partnership, where philanthropists work alongside scientists and healthcare professionals to address pressing health challenges. The narratives become a source of inspiration for individuals seeking to maximize the impact of their contributions, emphasizing the potential for collaborative efforts to drive meaningful progress in medical research.

Addressing Health Disparities: A Focus on Inclusive Research

Some narratives within this theme unfold stories of individuals who, in their commitment to funding research, prioritized initiatives aimed at addressing health disparities. These individuals recognized that not all communities have equal access to healthcare resources or benefit from advancements in medical research, and their philanthropic efforts were directed at fostering inclusivity in research endeavors.

Addressing health disparities involves a commitment to equity, with a focus on ensuring that the benefits of medical research are accessible to all segments of the population. The narratives become a guide for individuals seeking to make a socially impactful contribution, illustrating that philanthropy in research can play a crucial role in promoting health equity and inclusivity.

Innovative Funding Models: Paving New Paths for Progress

The commitment to funding research sometimes involves innovative funding models—exploring new paths for progress beyond traditional avenues. The narratives within this theme share stories of individuals who, driven by a spirit of innovation, sought creative and novel approaches to fund research initiatives, breaking new ground in the philanthropic landscape.

Innovative funding models involve a willingness to explore unconventional avenues, whether through partnerships, crowdfunding, or novel financial instruments. The narratives become a source of inspiration for individuals seeking to make a unique and impactful contribution, emphasizing the potential for creativity and innovation to drive transformative change in the field of medical research.

Advocacy for Research Funding: Influencing Policy and Public Perception

Some narratives within this theme unfold stories of individuals who, in addition to their financial contributions, became advocates for research funding—working to influence policy decisions and public perception regarding the importance of investing in medical research. These individuals recognized the interconnected nature of philanthropy, advocacy, and policy in shaping the landscape of healthcare and research.

Advocacy for research funding involves a commitment to raising awareness, mobilizing support, and engaging with policymakers to prioritize research initiatives. The narratives become a guide for individuals seeking to create systemic change, illustrating that advocacy can be a powerful complement to financial contributions in the effort to advance medical knowledge and improve healthcare outcomes.

Data Sharing Initiatives: Contributing to Collaborative Knowledge

In the commitment to funding research, some narratives share stories of individuals who actively supported data sharing initiatives. Recognizing the value of collaborative knowledge, these individuals contributed to initiatives that promote the sharing of research data, fostering a culture of openness and collaboration in the scientific community.

Data sharing initiatives involve a commitment to transparency and collective learning, allowing researchers to build upon existing knowledge and accelerate the pace of discoveries. The narratives become a guide for individuals interested in contributing to the collaborative nature of medical research, emphasizing the importance of creating a shared repository of information for the benefit of the scientific community and society at large.

Global Health Initiatives: Extending Impact Beyond Borders

In the commitment to funding research, some individuals directed their efforts towards global health initiatives—recognizing that health challenges extend beyond regional boundaries. The narratives within this theme share stories of individuals who, through their philanthropic endeavors, sought to address pressing global health issues and contribute to research initiatives with a broad and far-reaching impact.

Global health initiatives involve a commitment to understanding and addressing health challenges on a global scale, recognizing the interconnectedness of health outcomes worldwide. The narratives become a source of inspiration for individuals seeking to make a global impact, illustrating that philanthropy in research can transcend geographical boundaries and contribute to the advancement of health on a global scale.

Evaluation and Impact Measurement: Ensuring Effective Contributions

The commitment to funding research is often accompanied by a dedication to evaluating and measuring impact. The narratives within this theme share stories of individuals who, recognizing the importance of accountability, actively engaged in assessing the effectiveness of their contributions, ensuring that their philanthropic efforts resulted in tangible advancements in medical knowledge and healthcare outcomes.

Evaluation and impact measurement involve a commitment to transparency and accountability, with a focus on understanding the real-world effects of philanthropic contributions. The narratives become a guide for individuals seeking to ensure the effectiveness of their efforts, emphasizing the importance of ongoing evaluation and adaptation in the dynamic landscape of medical research.

Conclusion: A Tapestry of Impactful Philanthropy in Medical Research

In the chapter on "Wellness Transformation Journeys," the narratives of commitment to funding research converge to form a tapestry of impactful philanthropy in medical research. As we immerse ourselves in the stories of individuals who, driven by personal experiences, dedicated themselves to advancing knowledge, we witness not only the transformative power of philanthropy but also the potential for individuals to actively shape the trajectory of medical research. Each narrative becomes a testament to the resilience of the human spirit and the profound impact that committed individuals can have on the advancement of medical knowledge and the improvement of healthcare outcomes.

Helping Others Find Wholeness

In the expansive realm of wellness transformation journeys, the subtopic "Helping Others Find Wholeness" weaves together narratives of individuals who, having navigated their own paths of healing and self-discovery, dedicated themselves to supporting and empowering others on their wellness journeys. This chapter explores stories of compassion, mentorship, and the transformative power of extending a helping hand to those seeking wholeness in the face of health challenges.

The Compassionate Journey: From Recipient to Provider of Support

The narratives within this theme share stories of individuals who, having experienced the transformative power of support during their own wellness journeys, felt compelled to pay it forward. These individuals transitioned from being recipients of compassion and guidance to becoming providers of support, recognizing the profound impact that empathy and understanding can have on the well-being of others facing health challenges.

The compassionate journey involves a shift in perspective—a realization that one's own healing journey can serve as a source of inspiration and support for others. The narratives become a testament to the transformative power of empathy and compassion, illustrating that the act of helping others find wholeness is not only an extension of kindness but also a catalyst for profound personal and collective growth.

Peer Mentorship: Walking Alongside Others on the Journey

Some narratives within this theme unfold stories of individuals who engaged in peer mentorship—establishing connections with others facing similar health challenges and providing a supportive presence on their wellness journeys. These individuals recognized the unique value of shared experiences and the impact of walking alongside others in their pursuit of wholeness.

Peer mentorship involves creating a community of support, where individuals can draw strength from shared experiences, challenges, and triumphs. The narratives become a guide for those interested in peer mentorship, emphasizing the importance of building connections, fostering a sense of belonging, and creating a supportive network for individuals navigating the complexities of their wellness transformation journeys.

Educational Advocacy: Empowering Through Knowledge

The narratives within this theme share stories of individuals who, in their commitment to helping others find wholeness, became advocates for education—empowering individuals with knowledge about their health conditions, treatment options, and strategies for overall well-being. These individuals recognized that access to information is a powerful tool in the journey toward wholeness.

Educational advocacy involves a commitment to disseminating accurate and accessible information, empowering individuals to make informed decisions about their health. The narratives become a source of inspiration for those interested in educational advocacy, illustrating that knowledge is a key component in the empowerment of individuals facing health challenges.

Support Group Initiatives: Fostering Community and Connection

Some narratives within this theme unfold stories of individuals who, driven by a desire to foster community and connection, initiated or participated in support group initiatives. These individuals recognized the importance of creating spaces where individuals facing similar health challenges could come together, share experiences, and find strength in a collective journey toward wholeness.

Support group initiatives involve a commitment to building a sense of community, where individuals can find understanding, validation, and encouragement. The narratives become a guide for those interested in creating or participating in support groups, emphasizing the transformative power of shared experiences and the sense of camaraderie that arises from collective support.

Advocacy for Accessibility: Breaking Barriers to Wellness Resources

The narratives within this theme share stories of individuals who, in their commitment to helping others find wholeness, became advocates for accessibility—working to break down barriers that hinder access to wellness resources, healthcare services, and support networks. These individuals recognized that disparities in access can profoundly impact an individual's ability to navigate their wellness journey.

Advocacy for accessibility involves a commitment to addressing systemic barriers, advocating for policy changes, and promoting inclusivity in wellness resources and services. The narratives become a source of inspiration for those interested in advocacy work, illustrating that the act of breaking down barriers is a crucial step in ensuring that all individuals have the opportunity to pursue wholeness.

Crisis Intervention: Providing Support in Critical Moments

Some narratives within this theme unfold stories of individuals who, recognizing the critical nature of certain moments in the wellness journey, engaged in crisis intervention—providing immediate support and assistance to individuals facing acute challenges in their health and well-being. These individuals understood the importance of timely and compassionate intervention in moments of crisis.

Crisis intervention involves a commitment to being present for individuals during moments of acute distress, offering support, and connecting them to appropriate resources. The narratives become a guide for those interested in crisis intervention, emphasizing the transformative impact of timely and empathetic support in critical moments of the wellness journey.

Holistic Wellness Workshops: Nurturing Mind, Body, and Spirit

The narratives within this theme share stories of individuals who, in their commitment to helping others find wholeness, organized and participated in holistic wellness workshops. These individuals recognized the interconnected nature of mind, body, and spirit and sought to provide comprehensive support that goes beyond addressing physical symptoms.

Holistic wellness workshops involve a commitment to nurturing all aspects of well-being, including mental, emotional, and spiritual dimensions. The narratives become a source of inspiration for those interested in organizing or participating in holistic wellness initiatives, emphasizing the transformative power of a holistic approach in supporting individuals on their journey toward wholeness.

Technological Innovations: Leveraging Tools for Support

Some narratives within this theme unfold stories of individuals who leveraged technological innovations to provide support and resources for those seeking wholeness. These individuals recognized the potential of technology to connect individuals, disseminate information, and create virtual communities that transcend geographical boundaries.

Technological innovations involve a commitment to exploring and utilizing digital tools to enhance accessibility and support in the wellness journey. The narratives become a guide for those interested in leveraging technology for wellness support, illustrating that innovative approaches can significantly impact the ability of individuals to connect and access resources on their path toward wholeness.

Creative Arts Therapy: Expressive Pathways to Wholeness

The narratives within this theme share stories of individuals who, in their commitment to helping others find wholeness, explored the transformative power of creative arts therapy. These individuals recognized the potential of expressive arts—such as music, visual arts, and dance—as pathways for individuals to explore and express their emotions on the journey toward healing.

Creative arts therapy involves a commitment to incorporating artistic and expressive modalities as tools for self-discovery, healing, and empowerment. The narratives become a source of inspiration for those interested in creative arts therapy, emphasizing the transformative and therapeutic potential of engaging in expressive arts on the path toward wholeness.

Integration of Complementary Therapies: A Holistic Approach

Some narratives within this theme unfold stories of individuals who, in their commitment to helping others find wholeness, integrated complementary therapies into their support initiatives. These individuals recognized the value of a holistic approach, incorporating practices such as acupuncture, meditation, and herbal therapies to complement traditional healthcare in the pursuit of well-being.

Integration of complementary therapies involves a commitment to offering a diverse range of approaches that address the physical, mental, and spiritual dimensions of wellness. The narratives become a guide for those interested in incorporating complementary therapies into their support initiatives, illustrating the potential for a holistic approach to support individuals on their journey toward wholeness.

Conclusion: The Continuum of Support in Wellness Transformation

In the chapter on "Wellness Transformation Journeys," the narratives of helping others find wholeness converge to illustrate the continuum of support in the realm of wellness transformation. As we immerse ourselves in the stories of individuals who, having experienced their own journeys, dedicated themselves to supporting others, we witness not only the transformative power of compassion and empathy but also the potential for collective support to shape and redefine the wellness journey for individuals facing health challenges. Each narrative becomes a testament to the resilience of the human spirit and the profound impact that individuals can have on the well-being and wholeness of others through acts of support, mentorship, and compassion.

Chapter 6: Environmental Activist Awakenings
Warnings Unheeded

In the tapestry of environmental activist awakenings, the subtopic "Warnings Unheeded" unfurls narratives of individuals who, attuned to the mounting environmental challenges, witnessed early signs and signals of ecological distress. This chapter delves into stories of awakening—the moment when individuals recognized the urgency of environmental issues and the consequences of unheeded warnings. These narratives illuminate the journey from awareness to activism, showcasing the transformative power of realizing the interconnectedness between human actions and the health of the planet.

Eco-Early Adopters: Recognizing the Signs of Change

The narratives within this theme share stories of individuals who, as eco-early adopters, were among the first to recognize the signs of environmental change. These individuals, whether scientists, researchers, or keen observers, noted shifts in ecosystems, climate patterns, and biodiversity that hinted at larger environmental issues. Their early recognition marked the beginning of an awakening—a pivotal moment when they understood the gravity of the situation and the potential consequences of unheeded warnings.

Eco-early adopters play a crucial role in sounding the alarm, acting as sentinels who bring attention to emerging environmental challenges. The narratives become a testament to the importance of keen observation, scientific inquiry, and the ability to connect disparate pieces of information to form a comprehensive understanding of the ecological landscape.

The Fragility of Ecosystems: Observing Disruptions in Balance

Some narratives within this theme unfold stories of individuals who, attuned to the fragility of ecosystems, observed disruptions in the delicate balance of nature. These individuals witnessed changes in species behavior, alterations in migration patterns, and shifts in the availability of resources—all indicative of the profound impact of human activities on the interconnected web of life.

Observing disruptions in the balance of ecosystems involves a heightened awareness of the intricate relationships that sustain life on Earth. The narratives become a guide for those interested in understanding the interconnectedness of ecological systems, emphasizing the need to recognize and address imbalances that can lead to far-reaching consequences for biodiversity and the health of the planet.

Climate Science Pioneers: Interpreting Data and Trends

The narratives within this theme share stories of climate science pioneers—individuals who, armed with data and scientific rigor, interpreted the trends that signaled impending environmental challenges. These individuals delved into climate science, atmospheric studies, and earth system research to unravel the complexities of climate change and its cascading effects on the environment.

Climate science pioneers contribute to the body of knowledge that informs our understanding of climate patterns, trends, and potential impacts. The narratives become a source of inspiration for those interested in climate science, illustrating the transformative power of rigorous scientific inquiry in unraveling the intricacies of the Earth's climate system.

Oceanographers and Ecologists: Uncovering Marine Distress Signals

Some narratives within this theme unfold stories of oceanographers and ecologists who, through their research, uncovered distress signals in marine ecosystems. These individuals observed phenomena such as coral bleaching, declining fish populations, and disruptions in ocean currents—a stark reminder of the vulnerability of the world's oceans to human-induced stressors.

Oceanographers and ecologists play a vital role in highlighting the interconnectedness between human activities and the health of marine environments. The narratives become a guide for those interested in understanding the impact of human actions on oceans, emphasizing the need for sustainable practices to preserve the rich biodiversity and ecological balance of marine ecosystems.

Botanists and Conservationists: Witnessing Habitat Decline

The narratives within this theme share stories of botanists and conservationists who, immersed in the study and preservation of plant life, witnessed the decline of habitats due to human activities. These individuals observed deforestation, habitat fragmentation, and the loss of biodiversity—indications of the broader ecological crisis unfolding on a global scale.

Botanists and conservationists serve as custodians of plant diversity, drawing attention to the importance of preserving habitats for the well-being of both flora and fauna. The narratives become a source of inspiration for those interested in plant conservation, illustrating the interconnected nature of ecosystems and the imperative to protect habitats to sustain life on Earth.

Indigenous Wisdom: Recognizing Disruptions in Traditional Knowledge

Some narratives within this theme unfold stories of individuals who, rooted in indigenous wisdom, recognized disruptions in traditional knowledge systems. These individuals observed changes in weather patterns, alterations in seasonal cycles, and shifts in animal behaviors—indicators that resonated with ancestral knowledge passed down through generations.

Indigenous wisdom holds a unique perspective on the environment, often grounded in a deep connection to the land and a profound understanding of ecological interdependencies. The narratives become a guide for those interested in integrating traditional knowledge into environmental discourse, emphasizing the importance of recognizing and respecting indigenous perspectives in addressing environmental challenges.

Early Environmental Activists: Advocating for Change

The narratives within this theme share stories of early environmental activists who, having witnessed the warnings unheeded, transitioned from passive observers to advocates for change. These individuals recognized that awareness alone was insufficient and that action was needed to address the root causes of environmental degradation.

Early environmental activists became the vanguard of a burgeoning movement, raising their voices to call for policy changes, conservation measures, and sustainable practices. The narratives become a testament to the transformative power of advocacy, illustrating that individuals can play a pivotal role in mobilizing communities, influencing policies, and effecting positive change in the face of environmental challenges.

Media and Communication Influencers: Amplifying Environmental Messages

Some narratives within this theme unfold stories of individuals in media and communication who, recognizing the urgency of environmental issues, dedicated themselves to amplifying messages of ecological importance. These individuals harnessed the power of storytelling, journalism, and media platforms to bring environmental issues to the forefront of public consciousness.

Media and communication influencers contribute to shaping public discourse, influencing attitudes, and catalyzing collective action. The narratives become a source of inspiration for those interested in leveraging communication for environmental advocacy, emphasizing the transformative impact of effectively conveying the urgency of environmental challenges to a wider audience.

Educational Initiatives: Fostering Environmental Awareness

The narratives within this theme share stories of individuals who, in response to warnings unheeded, initiated educational initiatives to foster environmental awareness. These individuals recognized the importance of educating communities, empowering individuals with knowledge, and inspiring a collective commitment to sustainable practices.

Educational initiatives involve a commitment to raising awareness, providing information, and nurturing a sense of environmental responsibility. The narratives become a guide for those interested in educational outreach, illustrating that transformative change begins with informed individuals who understand the impact of their actions on the environment.

Scientific Advocacy: Bridging Research and Policy

Some narratives within this theme unfold stories of individuals who, armed with scientific expertise, engaged in scientific advocacy to bridge the gap between research findings and policy action. These individuals recognized the need for evidence-based decision-making and worked to translate scientific knowledge into policies that address environmental challenges.

Scientific advocacy involves a commitment to ensuring that research findings inform policy decisions, leading to effective strategies for environmental conservation. The narratives become a source of inspiration for those interested in the intersection of science and policy, emphasizing the transformative power of aligning research efforts with actionable policies to address urgent environmental issues.

Conclusion: From Awareness to Action in Environmental Activism

In the chapter on "Environmental Activist Awakenings," the narratives of warnings unheeded converge to illuminate the journey from awareness to action in environmental activism. As we immerse ourselves in the stories of individuals who, having witnessed early signs of environmental distress, transitioned to advocates for change, we witness not only the transformative power of awareness but also the imperative of taking meaningful action to address the interconnected challenges facing the planet. Each narrative becomes a testament to the resilience of the human spirit and the potential for individuals to contribute to a more sustainable and harmonious relationship with the natural world.

Devastation Witnessed

In the continuum of environmental activist awakenings, the subtopic "Devastation Witnessed" unfurls narratives of individuals who, confronted with the stark realities of environmental degradation, witnessed firsthand the profound impact of human activities on the planet. This chapter delves into stories of witnessing ecological devastation—the moment when individuals, with eyes wide open, saw the destruction of ecosystems, habitats, and biodiversity, compelling them to embark on a journey of environmental advocacy and activism.

Decimation of Biodiversity: A Silent Crisis Unfolding

The narratives within this theme share stories of individuals who, deeply attuned to the intricate tapestry of life on Earth, witnessed the decimation of biodiversity—a silent crisis unfolding in the face of habitat destruction, pollution, and climate change. These individuals observed the disappearance of species, the loss of ecosystems, and the unraveling of the delicate balance that sustains life.

The decimation of biodiversity involves a profound recognition of the interconnectedness between species and ecosystems. The narratives become a guide for those interested in understanding the far-reaching consequences of biodiversity loss, emphasizing the urgent need to address the root causes of this silent crisis to preserve the richness and resilience of Earth's ecosystems.

Vanishing Wilderness: The Encroachment of Human Activities

Some narratives within this theme unfold stories of individuals who, venturing into once-pristine wilderness areas, witnessed the encroachment of human activities—deforestation, urbanization, and resource exploitation. These individuals saw firsthand the transformation of untouched landscapes into zones marked by the imprint of human presence, a stark reminder of the impact of expanding human populations on the natural world.

The vanishing wilderness involves a visceral experience of witnessing the transformation of untouched landscapes into areas altered by human activities. The narratives become a source of inspiration for those interested in wilderness conservation, illustrating the transformative power of recognizing the intrinsic value of untouched ecosystems and the imperative to protect these areas from further degradation.

Ravages of Deforestation: A Landscape Stripped Bare

The narratives within this theme share stories of individuals who, amidst the vast expanses of forests, witnessed the ravages of deforestation—a landscape stripped bare by logging, agricultural expansion, and infrastructure development. These individuals saw the once-lush canopies reduced to barren landscapes, the repercussions of which extend beyond the loss of trees to impact climate, biodiversity, and local communities.

The ravages of deforestation involve a direct encounter with the consequences of exploiting one of Earth's most vital ecosystems. The narratives become a guide for those interested in understanding the interconnected nature of deforestation and its cascading effects on the planet, emphasizing the need for sustainable forest management and conservation efforts.

Dying Coral Reefs: A Bleak Underwater Reality

Some narratives within this theme unfold stories of individuals who, exploring the vibrant underwater realms, witnessed the dying coral reefs—a bleak reality marked by coral bleaching, ocean acidification, and the deterioration of marine ecosystems. These individuals saw the vibrant colors of coral colonies fade, replaced by the stark whiteness of bleached skeletons, signaling the fragile state of the world's coral reefs.

The dying coral reefs involve a poignant recognition of the vulnerability of marine ecosystems to the impacts of climate change and human activities. The narratives become a source of inspiration for those interested in marine conservation, illustrating the transformative power of acknowledging the intricate beauty and ecological significance of coral reefs and the urgent need to protect these underwater wonders.

Pollution Pervasiveness: A World Contaminated

The narratives within this theme share stories of individuals who, traversing urban landscapes and natural environments alike, witnessed the pervasiveness of pollution—a world contaminated by industrial discharge, plastic waste, and chemical pollutants. These individuals observed the visible and invisible manifestations of pollution, recognizing the threats posed to ecosystems, wildlife, and human health.

The pervasiveness of pollution involves a stark confrontation with the consequences of unsustainable consumption and industrial practices. The narratives become a guide for those interested in addressing environmental pollution, emphasizing the transformative power of recognizing the interconnected nature of pollution and the need for collective action to mitigate its impacts on the planet.

Human-Wildlife Conflict: Encounters with Disrupted Ecosystems

Some narratives within this theme unfold stories of individuals who, navigating areas where human and wildlife territories intersect, witnessed the complexities of human-wildlife conflict—an encounter with disrupted ecosystems where human activities encroach upon natural habitats, leading to conflicts between people and wildlife. These individuals saw the challenges faced by both human communities and wildlife as they navigated shared spaces.

Human-wildlife conflict involves a nuanced understanding of the challenges arising from habitat fragmentation and the need for sustainable coexistence between humans and wildlife. The narratives become a source of inspiration for those interested in conservation efforts that address the complexities of preserving biodiversity while safeguarding the well-being of local communities.

Arctic Meltdown: The Accelerated Retreat of Ice

The narratives within this theme share stories of individuals who, witnessing the Arctic landscape, observed the accelerated retreat of ice—a manifestation of climate change with far-reaching implications for global sea levels, ecosystems, and weather patterns. These individuals saw the shrinking ice sheets, the thinning of sea ice, and the dramatic changes in the Arctic environment.

The Arctic meltdown involves a sobering acknowledgment of the rapid changes occurring in one of the world's most vulnerable and vital regions. The narratives become a guide for those interested in climate action, illustrating the transformative power of recognizing the interconnectedness of the Arctic with global climate systems and the imperative to address the root causes of ice loss.

Industrial Impact: Witnessing the Footprint of Extraction

Some narratives within this theme unfold stories of individuals who, standing at the peripheries of industrial zones, witnessed the footprint of extraction—a landscape scarred by mining, oil drilling, and resource exploitation. These individuals saw the ecological disruptions and social consequences of industrial activities, recognizing the need for responsible and sustainable resource management.

The industrial impact involves a direct confrontation with the consequences of resource extraction on ecosystems, communities, and biodiversity. The narratives become a source of inspiration for those interested in advocating for responsible resource management, emphasizing the transformative power of recognizing the ecological limits of industrial activities and the importance of transitioning toward sustainable practices.

Urban Expansion: Concrete Jungles Encroaching Nature

The narratives within this theme share stories of individuals who, amidst urban landscapes, witnessed the relentless march of urban expansion—concrete jungles encroaching upon natural habitats, green spaces, and ecosystems. These individuals saw the transformation of once-natural landscapes into urban environments, recognizing the challenges posed to biodiversity, air quality, and the overall well-being of urban communities.

Urban expansion involves a recognition of the environmental impacts of rapid urbanization and the need for sustainable urban development. The narratives become a guide for those interested in urban planning and environmental conservation within urban areas, emphasizing the transformative power of recognizing the importance of balancing urban growth with ecological preservation.

Conclusion: From Witnessing Devastation to Environmental Advocacy

In the chapter on "Environmental Activist Awakenings," the narratives of devastation witnessed converge to illustrate the journey from witnessing the profound impact of environmental degradation to becoming advocates for change. As we immerse ourselves in the stories of individuals who, with eyes wide open, witnessed ecological devastation, we witness not only the transformative power of firsthand experience but also the imperative of translating that experience into meaningful action to address the interconnected challenges facing the planet. Each narrative becomes a testament to the resilience of the human spirit and the potential for individuals to contribute to a more sustainable and harmonious relationship with the natural world through environmental advocacy and activism.

Power of Protest

In the tapestry of environmental activist awakenings, the subtopic "Power of Protest" unveils narratives of individuals who, fueled by a passion for environmental justice, harnessed the transformative force of protest to amplify their voices and catalyze change. This chapter delves into stories of protest—the mobilization of communities, the confrontation of power structures, and the collective assertion of the right to a sustainable and ecologically balanced world.

Seeds of Dissent: From Individual Concerns to Collective Action

The narratives within this theme share stories of individuals who, initially driven by personal concerns and a sense of urgency, planted the seeds of dissent that would later blossom into movements for environmental change. These individuals, whether inspired by witnessing local environmental degradation or confronting global ecological crises, recognized the power of collective action to address the root causes of environmental issues.

Seeds of dissent involve a personal awakening that evolves into a shared conviction, fostering a sense of solidarity among individuals with a common cause. The narratives become a guide for those interested in sparking grassroots movements, emphasizing the transformative power of recognizing the collective agency of communities in effecting environmental change.

Local Activism: Protecting the Places We Call Home

Some narratives within this theme unfold stories of individuals who, motivated by a commitment to protect their local environments, engaged in grassroots activism within their communities. These individuals recognized that environmental issues often have immediate and tangible impacts on local ecosystems, communities, and well-being.

Local activism involves a dedication to addressing environmental challenges at the community level, where individuals can directly witness the effects of their efforts. The narratives become a source of inspiration for those interested in local environmental activism, illustrating the transformative power of community-driven initiatives in safeguarding the places we call home.

Youth-Led Movements: The Rise of Environmental Warriors

The narratives within this theme share stories of youth-led movements that emerged as powerful forces in the realm of environmental activism. Driven by a sense of urgency and a commitment to shaping their own futures, young activists around the world mobilized to demand environmental justice, climate action, and sustainable policies.

Youth-led movements involve a recognition of the unique perspectives and energies that young activists bring to environmental advocacy. The narratives become a guide for those interested in empowering and amplifying the voices of the next generation, emphasizing the transformative power of youth-led initiatives in driving the environmental agenda forward.

Indigenous Activism: Defending Sacred Lands and Wisdom

Some narratives within this theme unfold stories of Indigenous activism—efforts led by Indigenous communities to defend their sacred lands, protect traditional knowledge, and resist the encroachment of extractive industries. These individuals recognized the interconnectedness between the preservation of Indigenous cultures and the protection of the Earth.

Indigenous activism involves a profound understanding of the sacred relationship between Indigenous peoples and their ancestral lands. The narratives become a source of inspiration for those interested in supporting Indigenous-led environmental movements, illustrating the transformative power of recognizing and respecting the wisdom embedded in Indigenous cultures.

Global Alliances: Building Bridges for Planetary Change

The narratives within this theme share stories of individuals and organizations that, recognizing the global nature of environmental challenges, formed alliances and networks to build bridges for planetary change. These alliances brought together diverse voices, expertise, and resources to tackle environmental issues on a broader scale.

Global alliances involve a commitment to transcending geographical boundaries and collaborating across sectors and disciplines. The narratives become a guide for those interested in fostering global collaborations for environmental sustainability, emphasizing the transformative power of collective action in addressing complex and interconnected challenges.

Civil Disobedience: Challenging the Status Quo

Some narratives within this theme unfold stories of individuals who, frustrated by the inertia of political and corporate systems, embraced civil disobedience as a form of protest. These individuals recognized the need to disrupt the status quo, challenge unjust policies, and make their dissent visible to catalyze change.

Civil disobedience involves a deliberate and nonviolent refusal to comply with laws or policies deemed unjust, with the aim of highlighting moral or ethical principles. The narratives become a source of inspiration for those interested in exploring civil disobedience as a tool for environmental activism, illustrating the transformative power of principled resistance in the pursuit of justice.

Strategic Litigation: Holding Power Accountable

The narratives within this theme share stories of individuals and organizations that, recognizing the legal avenues available for environmental advocacy, engaged in strategic litigation to hold powerful entities accountable for environmental harm. These individuals understood the potential of legal action to compel change, establish precedents, and protect the rights of communities and ecosystems.

Strategic litigation involves a careful and purposeful use of legal tools to advance environmental justice. The narratives become a guide for those interested in exploring legal avenues for environmental advocacy, emphasizing the transformative power of using the law as a tool for holding power accountable and securing justice for affected communities.

Media Campaigns: Shaping Narratives for Impact

Some narratives within this theme unfold stories of individuals who, understanding the power of storytelling and media, engaged in impactful campaigns to shape public narratives and garner support for environmental causes. These individuals recognized the potential of media—whether traditional or digital—to raise awareness, influence public opinion, and mobilize communities.

Media campaigns involve a strategic use of communication tools to convey compelling narratives that resonate with diverse audiences. The narratives become a source of inspiration for those interested in leveraging media for environmental advocacy, illustrating the transformative power of storytelling in shaping perceptions and mobilizing collective action.

Consumer Activism: Voting with Wallets for Sustainability

The narratives within this theme share stories of individuals who, recognizing the role of consumer choices in driving environmental impact, engaged in consumer activism to promote sustainability and ethical practices. These individuals understood that economic decisions, from purchasing choices to investment decisions, can influence corporate behavior and industry practices.

Consumer activism involves a conscious effort to align economic choices with environmental values and principles. The narratives become a guide for those interested in advocating for sustainability through consumer actions, emphasizing the transformative power of collective consumer choices in driving positive change in industries and markets.

Conclusion: The Resilience of the Collective Voice

In the chapter on the "Power of Protest," the narratives of environmental activism converge to illuminate the resilience of the collective voice in driving change. As we immerse ourselves in the stories of individuals who, fueled by a passion for environmental justice, harnessed the transformative force of protest, we witness not only the power of collective action but also the imperative of ongoing advocacy to address the interconnected challenges facing the planet. Each narrative becomes a testament to the resilience of the human spirit and the potential for individuals, united in purpose, to contribute to a more sustainable and harmonious relationship with the natural world.

Sustainability as Mission

In the intricate tapestry of environmental activist awakenings, the subtopic "Sustainability as Mission" unfolds narratives of individuals and organizations that embraced sustainability not just as a goal but as a fundamental mission. This chapter delves into stories where sustainability becomes a guiding principle, a transformative force shaping decisions, practices, and initiatives to foster a harmonious relationship between humanity and the planet.

Foundations of Sustainable Practices: Ethical Frameworks for Action

The narratives within this theme share stories of individuals and organizations that, recognizing the need for ethical and sustainable practices, laid the foundations for a mission centered on principles of environmental responsibility. These pioneers understood that sustainability involves aligning actions with long-term ecological well-being and social equity.

Foundations of sustainable practices involve a commitment to ethical frameworks that guide decision-making, operations, and engagements. The narratives become a guide for those interested in integrating sustainability into their personal or organizational mission, emphasizing the transformative power of ethical foundations in driving meaningful change.

Corporate Stewardship: Rethinking Business for Long-Term Impact

Some narratives within this theme unfold stories of businesses and entrepreneurs who, awakening to the environmental challenges posed by traditional business models, embraced corporate stewardship as a mission. These visionaries recognized that businesses can be powerful agents of change, contributing to both profit and planet through sustainable practices.

Corporate stewardship involves a paradigm shift in the way businesses operate, with a focus on environmental and social responsibility. The narratives become a source of inspiration for those interested in redefining business for long-term impact, illustrating the transformative power of aligning corporate missions with sustainability goals.

Regenerative Agriculture: Nurturing the Earth for Future Harvests

The narratives within this theme share stories of individuals and communities that, realizing the ecological impact of conventional agriculture, embraced regenerative agriculture as a mission. These stewards of the land recognized the potential of agriculture not only to produce food but also to regenerate ecosystems, enhance soil health, and promote biodiversity.

Regenerative agriculture involves a commitment to nurturing the earth for future generations, acknowledging the interconnectedness between agricultural practices and environmental well-being. The narratives become a guide for those interested in sustainable farming practices, emphasizing the transformative power of regenerative agriculture in fostering a healthier planet.

Circular Economy Advocates: Reducing Waste, Maximizing Resources

Some narratives within this theme unfold stories of individuals and organizations that, confronted by the linear and wasteful nature of traditional economies, championed the circular economy as a mission. These advocates recognized the potential of creating systems where resources are used efficiently, waste is minimized, and products are designed for longevity and recyclability.

Circular economy advocacy involves a commitment to reimagining economic systems with sustainability at their core. The narratives become a source of inspiration for those interested in reducing waste and maximizing resources, illustrating the transformative power of circular economy principles in creating a regenerative and sustainable world.

Green Architecture: Building with Nature in Mind

The narratives within this theme share stories of architects and builders who, awakening to the environmental impact of traditional construction, embraced green architecture as a mission. These visionaries recognized that the built environment can coexist harmoniously with nature, incorporating sustainable materials, energy-efficient design, and ecological considerations.

Green architecture involves a commitment to building with nature in mind, prioritizing environmental responsibility in every stage of the architectural process. The narratives become a guide for those interested in sustainable building practices, emphasizing the transformative power of green architecture in creating spaces that enhance both human well-being and ecological health.

Renewable Energy Champions: Powering the Future Sustainably

Some narratives within this theme unfold stories of individuals and organizations that, acknowledging the environmental consequences of fossil fuels, championed renewable energy as a mission. These advocates recognized the potential of harnessing the power of sun, wind, and water to meet energy needs sustainably and reduce reliance on finite resources.

Renewable energy champions involve a commitment to transitioning to cleaner and more sustainable sources of energy. The narratives become a source of inspiration for those interested in advancing renewable energy solutions, illustrating the transformative power of sustainable energy initiatives in mitigating climate change and promoting a greener future.

Conservationist Entrepreneurs: Balancing Profit with Biodiversity

The narratives within this theme share stories of entrepreneurs who, driven by a passion for nature and wildlife, integrated conservation into their business missions. These trailblazers recognized that economic ventures can coexist with biodiversity conservation, promoting sustainable practices that benefit both ecosystems and local communities.

Conservationist entrepreneurs involve a commitment to balancing profit with the protection of natural habitats and species. The narratives become a guide for those interested in entrepreneurship with a conservation focus, emphasizing the transformative power of business models that prioritize ecological well-being.

Ocean Guardians: Preserving Marine Ecosystems

Some narratives within this theme unfold stories of individuals and organizations that, confronted by the degradation of marine ecosystems, took on the role of ocean guardians with a mission to preserve and protect the world's oceans. These stewards of the seas recognized the critical importance of healthy marine environments for global biodiversity and climate regulation.

Ocean guardians involve a commitment to safeguarding marine ecosystems through conservation, sustainable practices, and advocacy. The narratives become a source of inspiration for those interested in marine conservation, illustrating the transformative power of individuals and organizations dedicated to preserving the vast and vital expanse of our oceans.

Community-Led Sustainability: Empowering Local Resilience

The narratives within this theme share stories of communities that, realizing the interconnectedness between local well-being and global sustainability, embraced community-led sustainability as a mission. These empowered communities recognized their agency in shaping sustainable practices, enhancing resilience, and fostering a sense of shared responsibility.

Community-led sustainability involves a commitment to grassroots initiatives that empower local communities to take charge of their environmental destiny. The narratives become a guide for those interested in community-driven sustainability, emphasizing the transformative power of local actions in contributing to the global mission of a sustainable future.

Conclusion: Sustainability as a Guiding Light

In the chapter on "Sustainability as Mission," the narratives converge to illuminate the transformative power of sustainability as a guiding light. As we immerse ourselves in the stories of individuals and organizations that embraced sustainability not just as a goal but as a fundamental mission, we witness not only the power of aligned values but also the imperative of making sustainability a guiding principle in every facet of life. Each narrative becomes a testament to the resilience of the human spirit and the potential for sustainability to shape a more harmonious relationship between humanity and the planet.

Chapter 7: Education Against Odds Stories
Barriers to Learning

In the realm of education against the odds, the subtopic "Barriers to Learning" unfolds narratives that delve into the challenges individuals face on their educational journeys. These stories illuminate the resilience of those who, despite facing formidable obstacles, navigated through the complexities of barriers to learning, demonstrating the transformative power of education in the face of adversity.

Economic Hardship: The Weight of Limited Resources

The narratives within this theme share stories of individuals and communities grappling with economic hardship as a significant barrier to learning. These stories illuminate the profound impact of limited resources on educational opportunities, as individuals navigate financial constraints, lack of access to educational materials, and the pressure to contribute to family income.

Economic hardship involves a complex interplay of socio-economic factors that hinder access to quality education. The narratives become a guide for those interested in understanding and addressing the challenges posed by economic barriers, emphasizing the transformative power of education as a tool for economic empowerment and breaking the cycle of poverty.

Discrimination and Prejudice: Navigating Bias in Educational Spaces

Some narratives within this theme unfold stories of individuals facing discrimination and prejudice as formidable barriers to their educational pursuits. These individuals confront biases based on factors such as race, gender, ethnicity, or socioeconomic status, navigating a complex landscape where systemic inequalities hinder their access to quality education.

Discrimination and prejudice create a hostile environment that impedes learning and personal development. The narratives become a source of inspiration for those interested in promoting inclusivity and diversity in educational spaces, illustrating the transformative power of education in dismantling discriminatory barriers and fostering an environment of equality.

Cultural and Language Barriers: Bridging Gaps in Education

The narratives within this theme share stories of individuals navigating cultural and language barriers that pose significant challenges to their educational journeys. These individuals grapple with the complexities of learning in environments where cultural differences and language disparities create hurdles to effective communication and understanding.

Cultural and language barriers involve the need for innovative approaches to education that recognize and respect diverse cultural perspectives and linguistic backgrounds. The narratives become a guide for those interested in fostering inclusive educational practices, emphasizing the transformative power of education in bridging cultural and language gaps.

Geographical Isolation: Education Beyond the Horizon

Some narratives within this theme unfold stories of individuals residing in geographically isolated areas, where the lack of accessible educational institutions poses a formidable barrier to learning. These individuals navigate the challenges of distance, limited infrastructure, and isolation, seeking education beyond the conventional boundaries of urban centers.

Geographical isolation calls for creative solutions to bring education to remote areas, overcoming logistical challenges and ensuring equal access to learning opportunities. The narratives become a source of inspiration for those interested in advocating for educational equity in geographically isolated regions, illustrating the transformative power of education in expanding horizons and overcoming spatial barriers.

Disabilities and Special Needs: Nurturing Inclusive Learning

The narratives within this theme share stories of individuals with disabilities or special needs who confront the barriers that hinder their access to inclusive and quality education. These individuals navigate a landscape where physical, cognitive, or sensory differences often lead to exclusion, requiring tailored approaches and accommodations to ensure equitable learning opportunities.

Disabilities and special needs call for a commitment to inclusive education that recognizes and accommodates diverse learning styles and abilities. The narratives become a guide for those interested in promoting accessible and inclusive educational environments, emphasizing the transformative power of education in nurturing the potential of every learner.

Lack of Educational Infrastructure: Building Foundations for Learning

Some narratives within this theme unfold stories of individuals and communities grappling with the lack of educational infrastructure as a significant barrier to learning.

These stories highlight the challenges posed by inadequate school facilities, shortage of qualified teachers, and the absence of essential resources needed for a conducive learning environment.

The lack of educational infrastructure demands advocacy for investments in building the foundations necessary for quality education. The narratives become a source of inspiration for those interested in educational development, illustrating the transformative power of education in advocating for improved infrastructure that enhances the learning experience for all.

Conflict and Crisis: Education Amidst Turmoil

The narratives within this theme share stories of individuals and communities navigating the complexities of conflict and crisis as formidable barriers to learning. These individuals seek education amidst turmoil, facing the disruptions caused by armed conflict, displacement, and humanitarian crises that threaten the stability of educational institutions and access to learning.

Conflict and crisis demand resilience and innovative solutions to ensure that education remains a priority even in the most challenging circumstances. The narratives become a guide for those interested in promoting education in crisis-affected areas, emphasizing the transformative power of learning in restoring a sense of normalcy and hope amidst adversity.

Gender Inequality: Breaking the Chains of Educational Bias

Some narratives within this theme unfold stories of individuals challenging gender inequality as a pervasive barrier to learning. These individuals confront societal norms and biases that limit educational opportunities based on gender, advocating for equal access to education and breaking the chains of gender-based discrimination in learning environments.

Gender inequality calls for a commitment to dismantling stereotypes and fostering environments that empower individuals of all genders to pursue education without constraints. The narratives become a source of inspiration for those interested in promoting gender equity in education, illustrating the transformative power of education in challenging and overcoming ingrained biases.

Conclusion: Education as a Beacon Through Barriers

In the chapter on "Barriers to Learning," the narratives converge to illuminate the transformative power of education as a beacon that guides individuals through formidable challenges. As we immerse ourselves in the stories of resilience, determination, and innovation, we witness not only the barriers faced but also the indomitable spirit that education ignites in overcoming those obstacles. Each narrative becomes a testament to the resilience of the human spirit and the potential for education to break down barriers, creating pathways to knowledge, empowerment, and a brighter future.

Perseverance Paving Opportunity

In the tapestry of education against the odds, the subtopic "Perseverance Paving Opportunity" unfolds narratives that shine a light on the tenacity of individuals who, against formidable challenges, persisted on their educational journeys, turning adversity into opportunity. These stories illuminate the transformative power of perseverance, resilience, and a relentless pursuit of learning in creating pathways to education amidst adversity.

The Long Road to Literacy: Overcoming Early Educational Hurdles

The narratives within this theme share stories of individuals who faced early educational hurdles, whether due to limited access to early childhood education or challenges in acquiring basic literacy skills. These individuals embarked on the long road to literacy, overcoming barriers to foundational education through sheer determination, often discovering the joy of learning against all odds.

The journey to literacy involves a recognition of the fundamental importance of foundational skills in unlocking educational opportunities. The narratives become a guide for those interested in addressing early educational challenges, emphasizing the transformative power of perseverance in paving the way for lifelong learning.

From Street to School: Education as a Pathway from Adversity

Some narratives within this theme unfold stories of individuals who, having experienced life on the streets, found education as a pathway to escape adversity. These individuals, often facing homelessness, poverty, or exploitation, discovered the transformative potential of education in providing not only knowledge but also a way out of dire circumstances.

The transition from street to school involves a commitment to creating educational opportunities for marginalized individuals, recognizing the role education plays in breaking cycles of poverty and vulnerability. The narratives become a source of inspiration for those interested in outreach and educational programs for at-risk populations, illustrating the transformative power of education in offering a pathway to a brighter future.

Overcoming Learning Disabilities: Triumphs in the Face of Challenges

The narratives within this theme share stories of individuals who confronted learning disabilities and challenges in traditional educational settings. These individuals navigated a landscape where the conventional structures of education often posed barriers, demonstrating that perseverance, tailored support, and alternative approaches can lead to triumphs over learning challenges.

Overcoming learning disabilities involves a commitment to inclusive education that recognizes and accommodates diverse learning styles and abilities. The narratives become a guide for those interested in promoting accessible and supportive educational environments, emphasizing the transformative power of perseverance in unlocking the potential of every learner.

Late Bloomers: Embracing Education Beyond Conventional Timelines

Some narratives within this theme unfold stories of individuals who embraced education beyond conventional timelines, whether due to family responsibilities, societal expectations, or personal circumstances that delayed their educational pursuits. These individuals exemplify the notion that it is never too late to learn and that perseverance can open doors to education at any stage in life.

Late bloomers in education involve a commitment to fostering lifelong learning opportunities, recognizing that individuals may embark on educational journeys at different points in their lives. The narratives become a source of inspiration for those interested in promoting adult education and continuous learning, illustrating the transformative power of perseverance in embracing education beyond traditional expectations.

Refugee Scholars: Learning Amidst Displacement

The narratives within this theme share stories of individuals and communities displaced by conflict, persecution, or humanitarian crises who, amidst the upheaval, found ways to continue their education. These refugee scholars faced the challenges of displacement and uncertainty, demonstrating that perseverance and a commitment to learning can thrive even in the most adverse conditions.

Refugee scholars involve a commitment to providing educational opportunities for displaced populations, recognizing the transformative power of education in restoring a sense of normalcy and hope amidst crisis. The narratives become a guide for those interested in supporting education for refugees, emphasizing the resilience and perseverance of individuals who strive for learning despite displacement.

Single Parents: Juggling Parenthood and Educational Dreams

Some narratives within this theme unfold stories of single parents who, despite the additional responsibilities of parenthood, pursued their educational dreams. These individuals juggled the demands of raising a family with the pursuit of knowledge, illustrating that perseverance and determination can create opportunities for personal and educational growth.

Single parents pursuing education involve a commitment to creating supportive environments that recognize and accommodate the unique challenges faced by individuals balancing parenting and educational responsibilities. The narratives become a source of inspiration for those interested in advocating for policies and programs that empower single parents to pursue education, emphasizing the transformative power of perseverance in creating opportunities for personal and familial advancement.

From Child Labor to Classroom: Breaking the Chains of Exploitation

The narratives within this theme share stories of individuals who, having experienced child labor and exploitation, broke free from the chains of economic servitude through education. These individuals, often facing circumstances where education seemed like a distant dream, persevered in their quest for knowledge, transcending the cycle of exploitation to embrace the liberating power of learning.

The transition from child labor to the classroom involves a commitment to eradicating child exploitation and creating educational opportunities for vulnerable populations. The narratives become a guide for those interested in advocating for child rights and education, emphasizing the transformative power of perseverance in breaking the chains of exploitation and fostering a brighter future for children.

Incarcerated Learners: Education Behind Bars

Some narratives within this theme unfold stories of individuals who, while incarcerated, found solace and transformation through education. These incarcerated learners navigated a system that often denies access to educational resources, demonstrating that perseverance in the pursuit of knowledge can be a catalyst for personal growth and rehabilitation.

Incarcerated learners involve a commitment to promoting educational opportunities within correctional facilities, recognizing the rehabilitative potential of education in breaking the cycle of incarceration. The narratives become a source of inspiration for those interested in advocating for educational reforms in the criminal justice system, emphasizing the transformative power of perseverance in fostering positive change.

Conclusion: The Triumph of Tenacity

In the chapter on "Perseverance Paving Opportunity," the narratives converge to illuminate the transformative power of tenacity in the face of formidable challenges. As we immerse ourselves in the stories of perseverance, resilience, and a relentless pursuit of learning, we witness not only the barriers faced but also the indomitable spirit that education ignites in creating opportunities and pathways to a brighter future. Each narrative becomes a testament to the triumph of tenacity, illustrating the potential of education to pave the way for personal growth, empowerment, and the realization of untapped potential.

Paying Fortune Knowledge Forward

In the tapestry of education against the odds, the subtopic "Paying Fortune Knowledge Forward" unfolds narratives that spotlight the individuals who, having surmounted significant educational challenges, became beacons of inspiration by dedicating themselves to sharing knowledge and uplifting others. These stories illuminate the transformative power of education not only as a personal triumph but as a force for positive change when shared generously with communities, creating a ripple effect of empowerment.

Mentorship and Guidance: Nurturing Future Leaders

The narratives within this theme share stories of individuals who, having overcome educational obstacles, chose to pay their fortune of knowledge forward through mentorship and guidance. These mentors recognized the transformative impact of personalized support and guidance, becoming beacons for others navigating the complexities of their educational journeys.

Mentorship involves a commitment to nurturing the potential of others, sharing experiences, and providing guidance to uplift future leaders. The narratives become a guide for those interested in mentorship programs, emphasizing the transformative power of sharing knowledge and wisdom in fostering the growth and success of others.

Community Learning Centers: Empowering Through Accessible Education

Some narratives within this theme unfold stories of individuals who, recognizing the challenges of educational access in their communities, established community learning centers. These centers became hubs of knowledge, providing accessible and inclusive educational opportunities for individuals facing barriers to traditional forms of learning.

Community learning centers involve a commitment to democratizing education, making it available to all members of a community. The narratives become a source of inspiration for those interested in community-driven educational initiatives, illustrating the transformative power of creating spaces where knowledge is shared, and learning is a collective endeavor.

Educational Advocacy: Breaking Systemic Barriers

The narratives within this theme share stories of individuals who, propelled by their own experiences of overcoming educational challenges, became advocates for systemic change. These educational advocates recognized the broader societal barriers that hinder access to quality education and dedicated themselves to breaking down these barriers through advocacy, policy initiatives, and community engagement.

Educational advocacy involves a commitment to addressing systemic inequalities, promoting policy changes, and creating an environment where education is equitable and accessible to all. The narratives become a guide for those interested in educational activism, emphasizing the transformative power of advocacy in creating lasting change within educational systems.

Scholarship Initiatives: Investing in Future Scholars

Some narratives within this theme unfold stories of individuals who, having experienced the transformative power of education, established scholarship initiatives to invest in the academic pursuits of others. These scholarship providers recognized the financial barriers that often accompany educational endeavors and sought to create opportunities for deserving individuals to access higher education.

Scholarship initiatives involve a commitment to financial inclusivity, recognizing that education should not be restricted by economic constraints. The narratives become a source of inspiration for those interested in establishing or contributing to scholarship programs, illustrating the transformative power of investing in the educational journeys of future scholars.

Online Learning Platforms: Democratizing Knowledge Globally

The narratives within this theme share stories of individuals who, leveraging the power of technology, created online learning platforms to democratize knowledge on a global scale. These platform creators recognized the potential of the internet in breaking down geographical barriers and providing individuals worldwide with access to quality educational resources.

Online learning platforms involve a commitment to leveraging technology for educational inclusivity, making learning opportunities available to anyone with an internet connection. The narratives become a guide for those interested in digital education initiatives, emphasizing the transformative power of online platforms in making knowledge accessible globally.

Educational Entrepreneurship: Innovating for Impact

Some narratives within this theme unfold stories of individuals who, combining their passion for education with entrepreneurial spirit, founded initiatives or businesses with an educational focus. These educational entrepreneurs recognized the need for innovative approaches to learning and created ventures that had a positive impact on educational access, quality, or delivery.

Educational entrepreneurship involves a commitment to innovation, recognizing that creative solutions can address persistent challenges in education. The narratives become a source of inspiration for those interested in educational startups, illustrating the transformative power of entrepreneurship in driving positive change within the educational landscape.

Community Outreach Programs: Bridging Gaps Locally

The narratives within this theme share stories of individuals who, understanding the unique needs of their local communities, initiated community outreach programs to bridge educational gaps. These outreach programs became catalysts for change, providing educational support, resources, and opportunities tailored to the specific needs of the communities they served.

Community outreach programs involve a commitment to understanding and addressing the unique challenges faced by local communities, fostering a sense of collective responsibility for education. The narratives become a guide for those interested in community-driven educational initiatives, emphasizing the transformative power of localized outreach in creating positive educational change.

International Educational Partnerships: Fostering Global Collaboration

Some narratives within this theme unfold stories of individuals or organizations that, recognizing the interconnectedness of the world, forged international educational partnerships to foster global collaboration. These partnerships became avenues for sharing resources, expertise, and knowledge across borders, enriching educational experiences and opportunities on a global scale.

International educational partnerships involve a commitment to breaking down geographical and cultural barriers, fostering collaboration for the betterment of education worldwide. The narratives become a source of inspiration for those interested in global educational initiatives, illustrating the transformative power of international collaboration in creating a more interconnected and enriched educational landscape.

Educational Content Creation: Sharing Knowledge Digitally

The narratives within this theme share stories of individuals who, leveraging digital platforms, became content creators to share educational content with a wide audience. These creators recognized the power of digital media in disseminating knowledge and embraced platforms such as blogs, podcasts, or YouTube to reach and educate diverse audiences.

Educational content creation involves a commitment to leveraging digital tools for knowledge dissemination, making educational content accessible to a global audience. The narratives become a guide for those interested in digital content creation for educational purposes, emphasizing the transformative power of sharing knowledge in the digital age.

Conclusion: The Enduring Legacy of Shared Knowledge

In the chapter on "Paying Fortune Knowledge Forward," the narratives converge to illuminate the enduring legacy of individuals who, having triumphed over educational challenges, dedicated themselves to sharing knowledge and uplifting others. As we immerse ourselves in the stories of mentorship, community initiatives, advocacy, and global collaboration, we witness not only the transformative power of education but also the profound impact that sharing knowledge can have on individuals, communities, and the world. Each narrative becomes a testament to the enduring legacy of those who pay their fortune of knowledge forward, creating a ripple effect of empowerment, inspiration, and positive change.

Elevating Forgotten Voices

In the rich tapestry of education against the odds, the subtopic "Elevating Forgotten Voices" weaves narratives that bring to light the stories of individuals and communities whose educational struggles have often been overlooked or silenced. These stories illuminate the transformative power of education not only in overcoming personal challenges but also in giving a voice to those whose narratives have been marginalized, creating a platform for empowerment, advocacy, and societal change.

Indigenous Wisdom: Reclaiming Cultural Narratives

The narratives within this theme share stories of individuals from indigenous communities who, despite historical injustices and systemic marginalization, reclaimed their cultural narratives through education. These individuals recognized the importance of preserving and celebrating their indigenous wisdom, languages, and traditions, contributing to the broader tapestry of human knowledge.

Reclaiming cultural narratives involves a commitment to recognizing and valuing the contributions of indigenous knowledge systems. The narratives become a guide for those interested in advocating for indigenous education, emphasizing the transformative power of education in reclaiming cultural identities and empowering marginalized voices.

Minority Perspectives: Diverse Experiences in Education

Some narratives within this theme unfold stories of individuals from minority groups who navigated the complexities of education while contending with the additional challenges of systemic bias and discrimination. These individuals, often facing hurdles based on race, ethnicity, religion, or other minority identities, sought to disrupt the status quo and create spaces where diverse perspectives were acknowledged and valued.

Elevating minority perspectives involves a commitment to fostering inclusive educational environments that reflect the diversity of human experiences. The narratives become a source of inspiration for those interested in promoting diversity and inclusion in education, illustrating the transformative power of education in amplifying the voices of marginalized communities.

Rural Realities: Navigating Education in Remote Areas

The narratives within this theme share stories of individuals from rural and remote areas who, despite geographical isolation and limited access to educational resources, pursued learning as a means of empowerment. These individuals recognized the importance of education in transcending the challenges of rural life and sought to bring attention to the unique struggles faced by those in remote communities.

Navigating education in remote areas involves a commitment to addressing the educational inequities experienced by rural populations. The narratives become a guide for those interested in advocating for educational initiatives that bridge the urban-rural divide, emphasizing the transformative power of education in addressing the specific needs of remote communities.

Migrant Voices: Education Amidst Transitions

Some narratives within this theme unfold stories of individuals and families who, as migrants, faced the challenges of educational transitions, adapting to new systems, languages, and cultural contexts. These individuals sought not only to overcome the hurdles of migration but also to advocate for the rights and educational needs of migrant communities.

Elevating migrant voices involves a commitment to recognizing the resilience of individuals amidst migration and creating inclusive educational environments for migrant populations. The narratives become a source of inspiration for those interested in promoting education for migrants, illustrating the transformative power of education in facilitating smooth transitions and empowering migrant communities.

LGBTQ+ Experiences: Advocacy Through Education

The narratives within this theme share stories of individuals from the LGBTQ+ community who, in the face of discrimination and marginalization, utilized education as a tool for personal growth and societal change. These individuals recognized the transformative potential of education in challenging stereotypes, fostering inclusivity, and advocating for the rights of the LGBTQ+ community.

Advocacy through education involves a commitment to creating safe and affirming educational spaces for LGBTQ+ individuals. The narratives become a guide for those interested in promoting LGBTQ+ inclusive education, emphasizing the transformative power of education in challenging societal norms and elevating the voices of the LGBTQ+ community.

Displaced Learners: Education in Refugee Contexts

Some narratives within this theme unfold stories of individuals who, as refugees or displaced persons, sought education as a means of resilience and rebuilding their lives. These individuals, often facing the trauma of displacement, recognized the importance of education in providing stability, hope, and a sense of normalcy amidst the upheaval of forced migration.

Elevating displaced learners involves a commitment to recognizing the unique educational needs of refugees and creating opportunities for learning in refugee contexts. The narratives become a source of inspiration for those interested in supporting education for displaced populations, illustrating the transformative power of education in restoring a sense of agency and dignity.

Intersectional Experiences: Navigating Multiple Identities

The narratives within this theme share stories of individuals who navigate the intersectionality of their identities, contending with overlapping challenges related to race, gender, disability, or other factors. These individuals recognize the importance of education in addressing the complex interplay of societal biases and advocating for inclusive and equitable educational practices.

Navigating intersectional experiences involves a commitment to recognizing and accommodating the diverse needs of individuals with multiple marginalized identities. The narratives become a guide for those interested in promoting intersectional inclusivity in education, emphasizing the transformative power of education in honoring the full spectrum of human experiences.

Elder Learners: Lifelong Education Across Generations

Some narratives within this theme unfold stories of individuals from older generations who, recognizing the value of lifelong learning, pursued education in their later years. These elder learners, often challenging age-related stereotypes, sought to break down barriers to education for individuals of all ages and contribute to a culture of continuous learning.

Elevating elder learners involves a commitment to promoting educational opportunities for individuals throughout their lives. The narratives become a guide for those interested in advocating for age-inclusive educational practices, emphasizing the transformative power of education in fostering a culture where learning is a lifelong journey.

Conclusion: A Symphony of Diverse Narratives

In the chapter on "Elevating Forgotten Voices," the narratives converge to create a symphony of diverse voices, each contributing to the broader melody of human experiences in education. As we immerse ourselves in the stories of indigenous wisdom, minority perspectives, rural realities, migrant voices, LGBTQ+ experiences, displaced learners, intersectional identities, and elder learners, we witness the transformative power of education in elevating the voices that have been overlooked or silenced. Each narrative becomes a testament to the resilience of individuals and communities, illustrating the profound impact that education can have in amplifying forgotten voices, fostering understanding, and creating a more inclusive and equitable world.

Conclusion

The Ripple Effects of Transformation

In the culmination of "Stories of Resilience: Journeys of Hope and Growth: Turning Points of Transformation," the concluding chapter, "The Ripple Effects of Transformation," delves into the profound and far-reaching impact that individual stories of adversity, resilience, and growth can have on communities, societies, and the world at large. As we reflect on the collective wisdom and inspiration drawn from the preceding chapters, we witness the transformative power of personal narratives in creating ripple effects that extend beyond individual journeys, shaping the fabric of our shared human experience.

The Transformative Alchemy of Personal Narratives

At the heart of the concluding chapter is the recognition of personal narratives as alchemical agents of transformation. Each story, woven into the tapestry of this book, represents a unique blend of challenges, triumphs, and the invaluable lessons distilled from lived experiences. These narratives, like alchemical ingredients, undergo a transformative process, transcending the individual to become catalysts for change, inspiration, and collective growth.

Catalyzing Empathy and Understanding

One of the profound ripple effects of sharing personal narratives is the catalyzation of empathy and understanding. As readers immerse themselves in the diverse stories presented throughout the book, they are invited into the lived experiences of individuals from various backgrounds, cultures, and walks of life. This immersive journey fosters empathy by allowing readers to see the world through the eyes of others, breaking down barriers of ignorance and fostering a deeper understanding of the human experience.

The ripple effect of empathy extends beyond the pages of the book, influencing how readers engage with the world around them. It prompts reflection on personal biases, challenges preconceived notions, and inspires a more compassionate and inclusive worldview. In this way, the alchemy of personal narratives transforms not only the storyteller and the reader but contributes to a broader cultural shift towards empathy and understanding.

Inspiring Collective Action

The stories of resilience, whether rooted in overcoming personal struggles or contributing to societal change, carry the potential to inspire collective action. As readers witness the transformative journeys of individuals who have tackled adversity head-on, there emerges a collective call to action—a recognition that positive change is not only possible but achievable through determined effort and a shared commitment to growth.

The ripple effect of inspiration manifests in the formation of community initiatives, advocacy movements, and collaborative efforts to address shared challenges. Readers, inspired by the stories within the book, may find themselves compelled to take tangible steps toward positive change in their communities. Whether it be volunteering, advocating for social justice, or initiating projects that uplift others, the transformative alchemy of inspiration catalyzes a ripple effect that extends far beyond the individual stories.

Breaking the Silence: Destigmatizing Adversity

Many of the stories within this book shed light on topics that are often shrouded in silence and stigma—mental health struggles, past traumas, societal discrimination, and more. The act of sharing these stories, of breaking the silence, is itself a transformative force with far-reaching implications.

The ripple effect of destigmatizing adversity is multifaceted. It fosters an environment where individuals feel seen and heard, reducing the isolation that often accompanies personal challenges. It encourages open conversations about mental health, trauma, and societal issues, paving the way for collective healing and understanding. By breaking the silence, the book contributes to a cultural shift that prioritizes compassion, empathy, and support for those facing adversity.

Cultivating a Culture of Resilience

Resilience, a recurring theme throughout the book, emerges as a central pillar in the construction of a culture capable of weathering life's storms. The narratives of individuals who have not only survived but thrived in the face of adversity serve as beacons of resilience, illuminating a path for others to follow.

The ripple effect of cultivating a culture of resilience is evident in the empowerment of individuals and communities to navigate challenges with strength and grace. It involves a shift in perspective, reframing setbacks as opportunities for growth and transformation. This cultural shift not only influences personal attitudes but contributes to the creation of communities that support and uplift each other in times of difficulty.

The Intersectionality of Transformation

An important aspect of the ripple effects of transformation is the recognition of intersectionality—the interconnected nature of individual and collective experiences. The stories presented in the book reflect the diversity of human identities, acknowledging that transformation is not a one-size-fits-all journey.

The ripple effect of embracing intersectionality is the fostering of inclusive spaces that honor the unique challenges faced by individuals with diverse identities. It prompts a reevaluation of systems and structures that perpetuate inequality, advocating for more equitable and accessible pathways for growth and success. By recognizing and celebrating the intersectionality of transformation, the book contributes to the creation of a world where everyone's journey is acknowledged and valued.

Conclusion: The Ever-Expanding Circles of Impact

As we conclude our exploration of "The Ripple Effects of Transformation," it becomes evident that the impact of personal narratives extends far beyond the confines of individual stories. The transformative alchemy of sharing, empathizing, inspiring, breaking silence, cultivating resilience, and embracing intersectionality creates ever-expanding circles of impact.

The ripple effects continue to reverberate through communities, societies, and the collective consciousness long after the final pages of the book are turned. Each reader, touched by the transformative power of these stories, becomes an agent of change, contributing to the ongoing narrative of resilience, hope, and growth.

In the grand tapestry of human existence, "Stories of Resilience" serves as a thread—one that, when woven into the larger narrative of our shared journey, enriches the fabric of our collective story. The ripple effects of transformation, like concentric circles expanding outward, remind us of the interconnectedness of our experiences and the profound potential for positive change that lies within each of us. As we carry these stories forward, may we continue to create ripples of transformation, weaving a narrative of resilience, hope, and growth that transcends time and resonates across generations.

Internal Rebirth Reflects External Change

In the culminating reflections of "Stories of Resilience: Journeys of Hope and Growth: Turning Points of Transformation," the concluding chapter, "Internal Rebirth Reflects External Change," delves into the symbiotic relationship between personal transformation and its profound impact on the external world. As we traverse the intricate narratives of growth, forgiveness, overcoming adversity, and the pursuit of dreams, a central theme emerges—the idea that the internal metamorphosis of individuals reverberates far beyond the boundaries of personal experience, catalyzing external change that resonates within communities, societies, and the broader human tapestry.

The Inner Landscape: A Crucible of Transformation

At the heart of this exploration lies an understanding of the internal landscape as a crucible of transformation. The stories within the book illuminate the depth of human resilience, the capacity for forgiveness, and the tenacity with which individuals confront and surmount adversity. These internal shifts, often born from the crucible of personal challenges, mark the beginning of a journey that extends well beyond the individual self.

The Power of Personal Healing

One of the significant ripples of internal rebirth is the transformative power of personal healing. Many stories within the book touch upon the profound healing that occurs when individuals confront and reconcile with their past, trauma, or inner conflicts. This internal healing, though deeply personal, radiates outward, influencing relationships, communities, and the broader societal fabric.

As individuals undergo processes of healing, they often become catalysts for collective healing. By breaking the cycles of pain and dysfunction within their own lives, they contribute to a ripple effect that extends into their relationships and communities. The power of personal healing, therefore, becomes a force capable of initiating a chain reaction of positive change that transcends individual boundaries.

Forgiveness as a Catalyst for External Harmony

Forgiveness, explored in various narratives, emerges as a transformative force that bridges the internal and external realms of human experience. The stories of individuals who navigate the complex terrain of forgiveness illustrate that letting go of resentment and embracing forgiveness is not only an act of personal liberation but a catalyst for external harmony.

Forgiveness, when internalized and embodied, becomes a powerful agent of change in relationships and communities. It has the potential to break the chains of intergenerational conflicts, dismantle cycles of retribution, and foster environments conducive to understanding and reconciliation. The ripple effect of forgiveness, therefore, becomes a testimony to the interconnectedness of personal choices and the broader harmony of the external world.

Overcoming Adversity: A Beacon for Others

The narratives of overcoming adversity showcase the resilience of the human spirit in the face of formidable challenges. The internal strength cultivated through these journeys becomes a beacon for others facing similar struggles. The individuals who triumph over adversity not only undergo a personal metamorphosis but also become sources of inspiration and empowerment for their communities.

The ripple effect of overcoming adversity is evident in the collective resilience that emerges within communities. By witnessing the transformative journeys of individuals who have faced and conquered adversity, others find solace, inspiration, and a roadmap for their own journeys. The stories become a collective narrative of hope and endurance, shaping the external landscape through the shared strength of those who have navigated the depths of adversity.

Chasing Dreams: A Call to Collective Action

The pursuit of dreams, a recurring theme in the book, is a testament to the human capacity for vision, ambition, and the pursuit of a purpose larger than oneself. The stories of dreamers who translate their aspirations into tangible reality demonstrate that personal dreams have the power to galvanize communities and spark collective action.

As individuals chase their dreams, they often find themselves at the forefront of movements, initiatives, and projects that contribute to the betterment of society. The internal conviction to pursue a dream becomes a rallying point for others who share similar aspirations, fostering a sense of collective purpose and shared vision. The ripple effect of chasing dreams, therefore, extends beyond personal accomplishment to become a catalyst for collective transformation.

Transformative Leadership: A Blueprint for Societal Change

Embedded within the narratives is the concept of transformative leadership—individuals who, through their personal growth, become leaders capable of steering societal change. Whether overcoming adversity, embracing forgiveness, or pursuing ambitious dreams, these leaders exemplify the interconnectedness of personal development and the external impact of visionary leadership.

The transformative leaders depicted in the stories become architects of societal change. They influence policies, shift cultural paradigms, and inspire others to engage in the collective pursuit of a better world. The ripple effect of transformative leadership, therefore, becomes a blueprint for societal change, illustrating how the internal qualities of leaders shape the external landscapes of communities and nations.

Collective Consciousness: Shaping a Shared Future

At the intersection of internal rebirth and external change lies the concept of collective consciousness—the shared beliefs, values, and aspirations that shape the trajectory of societies. The stories within the book illuminate how individual transformations contribute to the evolution of collective consciousness, influencing the narratives and norms that define the shared experience of communities.

As individuals undergo internal rebirths, challenging and reshaping their own beliefs and perspectives, they contribute to a broader shift in collective consciousness. The ripple effect of these individual transformations is reflected in the changing narratives around issues such as resilience, forgiveness, and the pursuit of dreams. The collective consciousness, therefore, becomes a dynamic and evolving entity shaped by the sum of individual transformations.

Conclusion: An Ever-Expanding Symphony of Change

In the concluding exploration of "Internal Rebirth Reflects External Change," the narratives converge to create an ever-expanding symphony of individual and collective transformation. The internal rebirths of forgiveness, healing, resilience, and visionary pursuits resonate as harmonies that reverberate beyond personal stories, weaving into the larger narrative of our shared human experience.

As individuals embark on journeys of internal rebirth, they become integral players in the orchestration of external change. The ripple effects of personal growth extend far beyond the individual, becoming integral notes in the symphony of societal and cultural evolution. The stories within the book become chapters in a larger narrative of human progress, illustrating how internal transformations, both subtle and profound, contribute to the ongoing melody of change that shapes our collective destiny.

May the exploration of "Internal Rebirth Reflects External Change" inspire a recognition of the interconnectedness of personal and societal evolution. As we navigate the complex interplay between inner landscapes and external realities, may we find resonance in the transformative power of individual stories, understanding that each internal rebirth contributes to the symphony of change that defines our shared journey through time.

Growth Mindsets Fuel Positive Progress

In the final reflections of "Stories of Resilience: Journeys of Hope and Growth: Turning Points of Transformation," the concluding chapter, "Growth Mindsets Fuel Positive Progress," delves into the transformative power of cultivating a mindset oriented towards growth and continuous development. As we traverse the diverse narratives of overcoming adversity, forgiveness, pursuing dreams, and navigating profound personal growth, a common thread emerges—the recognition that a growth mindset serves as the catalyst for positive progress, both on an individual and collective level.

Understanding the Growth Mindset

At the heart of this exploration lies an understanding of the growth mindset—a belief system that sees challenges as opportunities for learning, embraces effort as the path to mastery, and views setbacks as a natural part of the learning process. The stories within the book exemplify the transformative impact of individuals who, faced with adversity, setbacks, or limitations, adopt a growth mindset, propelling them towards positive progress.

Embracing Challenges as Opportunities

A central tenet of the growth mindset is the view that challenges are not obstacles but opportunities for learning and growth. Many narratives within the book illustrate how individuals, when confronted with adversity, approached it not as a roadblock but as a stepping stone. This mindset shift becomes a driving force for positive progress, as challenges are reframed as valuable experiences that contribute to personal and collective development.

The individuals who embody this mindset become architects of their own growth, utilizing challenges as platforms for honing skills, deepening understanding, and cultivating resilience. The ripple effect of embracing challenges as opportunities is evident in the unfolding narratives of individuals who, through their growth-oriented perspective, inspire others to view challenges not with fear, but with a sense of possibility.

Effort as the Path to Mastery

A growth mindset emphasizes the importance of effort in the pursuit of mastery. The stories within the book highlight individuals who, recognizing the value of sustained effort and dedication, embark on journeys of continuous improvement. Whether in the face of professional challenges, personal transformations, or entrepreneurial endeavors, these individuals exemplify the belief that progress is achieved through persistent effort.

The growth mindset challenges the notion of innate talent and underscores the role of effort in achieving excellence. This perspective becomes a driving force for positive progress, as individuals commit to the ongoing process of learning, refining their skills, and evolving in alignment with their goals. The ripple effect of valuing effort as the path to mastery extends beyond personal achievements, influencing the broader culture towards a collective commitment to continuous improvement.

Viewing Setbacks as Learning Opportunities

Setbacks, rather than being viewed as failures, are embraced as integral components of the learning process within the growth mindset. The narratives within the book illuminate how individuals, when faced with setbacks, approached them not with defeatism but with a curiosity for understanding, learning, and adapting.

The growth mindset transforms setbacks into learning opportunities, extracting valuable insights from failures and using them as stepping stones for future success. This adaptive and resilient approach becomes a catalyst for positive progress, as individuals and communities evolve in response to challenges rather than being hindered by them. The ripple effect of viewing setbacks as learning opportunities is seen in the narratives of individuals who, having navigated setbacks with resilience and perseverance, inspire others to adopt a similar mindset in their pursuit of progress.

Encouraging a Culture of Lifelong Learning

A growth mindset inherently aligns with the concept of lifelong learning—a commitment to continuous development and the acquisition of knowledge throughout one's life. The narratives within the book showcase individuals who, irrespective of age or circumstance, embrace the idea that learning is a lifelong journey.

The growth-oriented perspective encourages a cultural shift towards valuing education and personal development at all stages of life. This cultural emphasis on lifelong learning becomes a driver for positive progress, as societies recognize the inherent value of an educated and adaptable populace. The ripple effect of encouraging a culture of lifelong learning is seen in the stories of individuals who, through their commitment to continuous growth, contribute to the creation of communities that prioritize education and intellectual curiosity.

Fostering Innovation and Creativity

A growth mindset serves as a fertile ground for innovation and creativity. The belief that intelligence and abilities can be developed through dedication and hard work unleashes a spirit of exploration and experimentation. The stories within the book illustrate how individuals, armed with a growth mindset, approached their endeavors with a sense of creativity, embracing the unknown and pushing the boundaries of what was deemed possible.

The growth mindset becomes a catalyst for positive progress, as innovation flourishes in environments where individuals are encouraged to take risks, learn from failures, and iterate on their ideas. The ripple effect of fostering innovation and creativity is evident in the narratives of individuals who, through their inventive approaches, inspire others to break free from conventional thinking and contribute to the positive evolution of their fields.

Promoting Resilience in the Face of Change

The adaptability inherent in a growth mindset becomes a cornerstone of resilience in the face of change. The narratives within the book portray individuals who, when confronted with dynamic and unpredictable circumstances, did not succumb to fear or resistance but embraced change as an opportunity for growth.

The growth mindset fosters resilience by instilling a belief in the capacity to navigate change, learn from new experiences, and adapt strategies as needed. This resilience becomes a force for positive progress, as individuals and communities weather challenges with a forward-focused mindset. The ripple effect of promoting resilience in the face of change is evident in the stories of individuals who, having embraced change as a constant, inspire others to approach uncertainty with a growth-oriented perspective.

Building Collective Momentum for Positive Change

At its essence, the growth mindset transcends individual narratives to become a collective force for positive change. The stories within the book illustrate how the adoption of a growth mindset, whether in personal relationships, professional endeavors, or community initiatives, creates a momentum that propels individuals and societies towards positive progress.

As individuals embrace the principles of a growth mindset, the collective impact is transformative. Communities that value learning, effort, and resilience become hubs of innovation, adaptability, and continuous improvement. The ripple effect of building collective momentum for positive change is seen in the narratives of individuals who, through their growth-oriented endeavors, contribute to the creation of environments that foster progress on a broader scale.

Conclusion: Nurturing a Growth Mindset for a Flourishing Future

In the exploration of "Growth Mindsets Fuel Positive Progress," the narratives converge to underscore the transformative potential of cultivating a growth-oriented perspective. As individuals adopt mindsets that embrace challenges, value effort, learn from setbacks, and prioritize continuous development, they become integral contributors to a collective narrative of positive progress.

May the stories within this book serve as testaments to the power of growth mindsets in fueling positive change. As we navigate the complex terrain of personal and collective development, may we be inspired by the narratives of resilience, learning, and adaptability. In nurturing a growth mindset, both individually and collectively, we embark on a journey towards a flourishing future where progress is not just an outcome but a continuous and shared endeavor.

THE END

Wordbook

Welcome to the glossary section of this book. Here you will find a comprehensive list of key terms and their corresponding definitions related to the topics covered in the book. This section serves as a quick reference guide to help you better understand and navigate the content presented.

key terms

1. Resilience: The ability to bounce back from adversity, challenges, or setbacks, demonstrating strength, adaptability, and perseverance.

2. Journeys of Hope and Growth: Personal experiences marked by a pursuit of positive change, development, and the aspiration for a better future.

3. Turning Points: Critical moments or events that mark a shift in direction, often leading to transformative personal or societal change.

4. Transformation: A profound and often fundamental change, encompassing shifts in mindset, behavior, and circumstances towards a more evolved state.

5. Adversity: Difficulties, hardships, or challenges that individuals face, often requiring resilience and strength to overcome.

6. Forgiveness: The act of pardoning or letting go of resentment, enabling emotional healing and personal growth.

7. Overcoming Obstacles: Successfully navigating and surmounting barriers or challenges in the pursuit of goals or personal development.

8. Embracing New Cultures: Openly accepting and integrating into unfamiliar cultural environments, fostering diversity and understanding.

9. Paying Traditions Forward: Transmitting cultural or familial practices, values, and wisdom to future generations or others in the community.

10. Career Transitions: Significant shifts or changes in one's professional path, often involving a move from one role or industry to another.

11. Discovering Hidden Passions: Uncovering latent interests or talents that ignite a newfound passion and purpose.

12. Acting on Purpose: Aligning actions with a clear sense of personal or societal purpose, leading to intentional and meaningful endeavors.

13. Imparting Hard-Won Wisdom: Sharing valuable insights gained through personal experiences, particularly those involving challenges and growth.

14. Spark of Business Idea: The initial inspiration or concept that ignites the creation of a new business venture or entrepreneurial pursuit.

15. Setbacks to Success: Challenges or obstacles encountered on the path to achievement, ultimately contributing to eventual success.

16. Leadership Through Crisis: Guiding and inspiring others with resilience and vision during times of difficulty or uncertainty.

17. Uplifting Local Communities: Engaging in actions that positively impact and empower the local community, fostering growth and well-being.

18. Despair to Hope: Transitioning from a state of hopelessness or distress to a renewed sense of optimism and possibility.

19. Redemption and Forgiveness: Seeking forgiveness and making amends after past mistakes, leading to personal and moral renewal.

20. Valuable Perspectives Gained: Acquiring new and insightful viewpoints through life experiences, contributing to personal growth.

21. Making Amends Through Service: Rectifying past wrongs or mistakes by actively engaging in service or acts of kindness.

22. Health Crises: Critical periods marked by challenges to physical or mental well-being, requiring resilience and commitment to recovery.

23. Commitment to Healing: A dedicated focus on recovering from health challenges, encompassing physical, mental, and emotional well-being.

24. Funding Research: Providing financial support for scientific or medical research initiatives aimed at advancing knowledge and finding solutions.

25. Helping Others Find Wholeness: Supporting and assisting individuals in their journey towards holistic well-being and fulfillment.

26. Warnings Unheeded: Ignoring or neglecting cautionary signs or advice, often resulting in negative consequences.

27. Devastation Witnessed: Experiencing the severe and widespread destruction of natural or human-made disasters.

28. Power of Protest: Utilizing organized and collective dissent as a means to advocate for social or political change.

29. Sustainability as Mission: Incorporating environmental responsibility and long-term resource conservation as a core organizational or personal objective.

30. Barriers to Learning: Obstacles or challenges that impede access to education or hinder the learning process.

31. Perseverance Paving Opportunity: Tenaciously persisting through challenges to create opportunities for oneself and others.

32. Paying Fortune Knowledge Forward: Sharing acquired knowledge, skills, or opportunities with others, contributing to their advancement.

33. Elevating Forgotten Voices: Amplifying the perspectives and experiences of marginalized or overlooked individuals or communities.

34. The Ripple Effects of Transformation: The far-reaching impacts and consequences that result from individual or collective transformative experiences.

35. Internal Rebirth Reflects External Change: The interconnected relationship between personal growth and its influence on broader societal or environmental shifts.

36. Growth Mindsets Fuel Positive Progress: The belief in continuous learning, resilience, and adaptability as drivers for individual and collective advancement.

Supplementary Materials

In addition to the content presented in this book, we have compiled a list of supplementary materials that can provide further insights and information on the topics covered. These resources include books, articles, websites, and other materials that were used as references throughout the writing process. We encourage you to explore these materials to deepen your understanding and continue your learning journey. Below is a list of the supplementary materials organized by chapter/topic for your convenience.

Introduction:

Brown, B. (2012). Daring Greatly: How the Courage to Be Vulnerable Transforms the Way We Live, Love, Parent, and Lead. Gotham.

Seligman, M. E. P. (2006). Learned Optimism: How to Change Your Mind and Your Life. Vintage.

Duckworth, A. (2016). Grit: The Power of Passion and Perseverance. Scribner.

Chapter 1: Immigrant Rebirth Stories:

Mukherjee, S. (2016). The Gene: An Intimate History. Scribner.

Nazario, S. (2007). Enrique's Journey. Random House Trade Paperbacks.

Li, Y. (2009). The Vagrants: A Novel. Random House.

Chapter 2: Tales of Professional Reinvention:

Pink, D. H. (2012). Drive: The Surprising Truth About What Motivates Us. Riverhead Books.

Bolles, R. N. (2019). What Color Is Your Parachute? 2019: A Practical Manual for Job-Hunters and Career-Changers. Ten Speed Press.

Newport, C. (2016). Deep Work: Rules for Focused Success in a Distracted World. Grand Central Publishing.

Chapter 3: Entrepreneurial Metamorphosis Stories:

Ries, E. (2011). The Lean Startup: How Today's Entrepreneurs Use Continuous Innovation to Create Radically Successful Businesses. Currency.

Guillebeau, C. (2012). The $100 Startup: Reinvent the Way You Make a Living, Do What You Love, and Create a New Future. Crown Business.

Christensen, C. M. (2013). The Innovator's Dilemma: When New Technologies Cause Great Firms to Fail. Harvard Business Review Press.

Chapter 4: Second Chance Tales:

Coelho, P. (2014). Manuscript Found in Accra. Vintage.

Kalanithi, P. (2016). When Breath Becomes Air. Random House.

Doyle, G. (2013). Carry On, Warrior: The Power of Embracing Your Messy, Beautiful Life. Scribner.

Chapter 5: Wellness Transformation Journeys:

Gawande, A. (2014). Being Mortal: Medicine and What Matters in the End. Metropolitan Books.

Pollan, M. (2018). How to Change Your Mind: What the New Science of Psychedelics Teaches Us About Consciousness, Dying, Addiction, Depression, and Transcendence. Penguin Press.

Mate, G. (2003). When the Body Says No: Understanding the Stress-Disease Connection. John Wiley & Sons.

Chapter 6: Environmental Activist Awakenings:

Klein, N. (2014). This Changes Everything: Capitalism vs. The Climate. Simon & Schuster.

Carson, R. (1962). Silent Spring. Houghton Mifflin.

Hawken, P. (2007). Blessed Unrest: How the Largest Movement in the World Came into Being and Why No One Saw It Coming. Viking.

Chapter 7: Education Against Odds Stories:

Tough, P. (2012). How Children Succeed: Grit, Curiosity, and the Hidden Power of Character. Mariner Books.

Davis, M. (2016). The Gift of Dyslexia: Why Some of the Smartest People Can't Read...and How They Can Learn. TarcherPerigee.

Gatto, J. T. (2005). The Underground History of American Education: A Schoolteacher's Intimate Investigation Into the Problem of Modern Schooling. Oxford Village Press.

Conclusion:

Dweck, C. S. (2006). Mindset: The New Psychology of Success. Random House.

Csikszentmihalyi, M. (2008). Flow: The Psychology of Optimal Experience. Harper Perennial.

Gladwell, M. (2008). Outliers: The Story of Success. Little, Brown and Company.

www.ingramcontent.com/pod-product-compliance
Lightning Source LLC
LaVergne TN
LVHW012037070526
838202LV00056B/5525